NO SEX,
NO SLEEP

NO SEX, NO SLEEP

SO YOU'RE GOING TO BE A FATHER

PAT FITZPATRICK

MERCIER PRESS
IRISH PUBLISHER - IRISH STORY

MERCIER PRESS

Cork

www.mercierpress.ie

© Pat Fitzpatrick, 2018

ISBN: 978 1 78117 532 3

10 9 8 7 6 5 4 3 2 1

A CIP record for this title is available from the British Library

Printed and bound in the EU.

FOR ROSE, FREDA AND JOE

CONTENTS

INTRODUCTION   9

1   YEAR ZERO – Things You Need to Know
                     Before Baby Comes   11
     1.1   What I'd Tell My Friends   11
     1.2   The Best Days of Your Life   27
     1.3   The Motherhood Effect   32
     1.4   Daddy Landmines   37
     1.5   What Kind of Dad Do You Want to Be?   42
     1.6   Time for a Change of Car   46
     1.7   Handling the Housework   50

2   THE BABY YEARS   55
     2.1   Surviving the Labour Ward   55
     2.2   What's in a Name?   60
     2.3   Bringing Baby Home   64
     2.4   Nappy Happiness   68
     2.5   Too Much Stuff   73
     2.6   Any Chance of Some Sex?   82
     2.7   Keep the Romance Alive   89
     2.8   Fence Mending   94
     2.9   Money Problems   97
     2.10 That's Weird!   103
     2.11 Dealing with Drowsy   107
     2.12 Mind Your Mind – Dad's Mental Health   113

3 THE TERRIBLE TWOS   **122**

    3.1   Toddler Survival Guide   122

    3.2   How's Your Christmas?   127

    3.3   Spring Cleaning in January   134

    3.4   Rain Pain   138

    3.5   Is it Really a Holiday?   146

    3.6   Embrace the Telly   159

    3.7   Time for School   164

    3.8   Can't Stand the Heat? Get into the Kitchen   168

    3.9   Do You DIY?   173

    3.10 Your Health Matters   178

4 THREENAGER   **183**

    4.1   Welcome to Your Threenager   184

    4.2   Oh Boy   188

    4.3   The Bedtime Story   192

    4.4   It's Potty Time   197

    4.5   How's Your Discipline?   203

    4.6   Can I Ask You a Question, Dad?   207

    4.7   The Restaurant   212

    4.8   School Time   217

    4.9   I Want to Cancel Mother's Day   220

INTRODUCTION

First of all, congratulations. You're going to be a dad. This is going to change your life in ways you can't imagine. Some of them are even good!

Jokes aside, a new child is going to rock your world, physically and emotionally. I want to give you a full flavour of what it's like, the lows as well as the highs. Most of the stuff I read before my kids came along focused on the amazing aspects of fatherhood. Looking back now, I wish someone had told me it isn't all leisurely walks with the buggy and trying to get them to say 'Dada' as their first word.

Your living room can be a lonely place at two in the morning, when you are pacing around trying to put your son to sleep. There is a sleep-deprived temptation to feel down about this and think you must be doing something wrong. You aren't. At some point in the next year you will end up walking the boards with a cranky child on your shoulder. It's part of your job.

As for losing the will to live in a restaurant because your kid has just spilled its second glass of apple juice on your pants – that also comes with the territory. Feel like crying because you've had two hours' sleep and you can't find your car keys? Snap. (Everything is lost, all the time, when you have kids.) Wondering if you made a big mistake and you'd do anything to get your old life back? It happens, but not for long.

Here's the thing. Kids are amazing. Mine are the best thing

that ever happened to me and I wouldn't hand them back for the world. (Not even for a naughty weekend in Berlin.) I'm sure every dad will tell you the same thing about his little home-wreckers.

But they're tough at the same time. I remember a friend telling me that his kids were fantastic, it was just a pity he was too tired to enjoy them. That's how it can feel sometimes. As if you are a spectator, thinking, *this is amazing, but I really need to go and have a lie down.*

I want this book to help you enjoy your kids as much as possible. For starters, you should know you are not alone, that we all struggle when there are kids under our feet. More than anything, I hope this book gives you a laugh. It's worth pointing out that I have written large parts of this tongue-in-cheek. That's another way of saying, don't sue me if you follow some piece of advice and your toddler gets stuck in the washing machine.

Honestly, I know as much about fatherhood as any other dad. I'd like to thank my amazing kids, Freda and Joe, for their patience as I learned on the job.

Above all, I'd like to thank my out-of-this-world wife, Rose, for teaching me pretty much everything I know about parenting. If it was left to me, my kids would still be wearing nappies and eating baby rice on their first day of college. Rose has done most of the planning when it comes to child-rearing; anything I did was just following orders.

One more thing. She asked me not to discuss our sex life in this book. So the title, *No Sex, No Sleep,* applies to other couples, not us. (If you must know, we're at it like rabbits.)

1

YEAR ZERO

THINGS YOU NEED TO KNOW BEFORE BABY COMES

1.1 WHAT I'D TELL MY FRIENDS

Ask any new parents what it's like to have kids and they'll tell you it's 'life-changing'. And then they'll lie down for a sleep in the middle of the road. Because as understatements go, life-changing is up there with 'you might feel a little bit tired'. Everything you thought you knew about yourself, your relationship and the real joys of five minutes alone is about to change. So it's as well to be prepared.

The problem is that nothing can really prepare you, because nothing compares to the first few years of parenthood. I remember feeling a bit bitter towards my buddies with kids, because they didn't warn me that the arrival of my daughter, Freda, would be like a tidal wave tearing into a small boat. Now that I'm on calmer shores, I can see that they were actually telling me, but I just didn't want to listen. When I told one friend about plans to write a novel once Freda was born, his reply was, 'You do realise your life is about to fall apart?' I thought he was just trying to scare me for a laugh.

To be honest, it's the conversations I had after the kids arrived that made the difference. That's when my friends told me that it's tough until your youngest reaches the age of four;

that it's not unusual to feel beaten down by the whole thing; that they found it hard going and there's nothing wrong with that. What we rarely say, because it hardly needs saying, is that we wouldn't even think of rolling back the clock. Because a few years of sleepless nights and red-raw nerves are a small price to pay for the pleasure of even five minutes with your kids, let alone half a lifetime.

But it's still worth knowing what's coming down the road. If I was trying to give a friend a flavour of life with new kids in the house, here's what I'd tell him.

You're Planless

Here is the problem with your plan for the child – you haven't got one. At least not compared to your partner. This will probably be used against you.

She is engaged in a project that makes the Apollo Space Program look like something they cobbled together over lunch. Your contribution was to sit through half an episode of *Supernanny,* while trying to keep a sneaky eye on Spartak Moscow vs Anderlecht on your phone. Worse again, you got caught.

It's not like you missed the fact that your partner was planning ahead. She started dragging you around buggy shops four hours after you stopped using contraception. Four months into the pregnancy, she started planning the meals she would use to wean the child off solids. That's planning a year ahead; you're not even sure what you are going to do tomorrow.

She did try to include you in the planning process by buying you a book called *Aaaaw, You're Going to Be a Dad*. You didn't read it. As a result, your plan is a vague notion of a trip to Old Trafford for the child's fourth birthday. You might be better to pretend you have no plan at all rather than admitting that.

In the meantime, I recommend you read through some online parenting advice forums. At least then you can get involved in conversations on baby-led weaning, wonder weeks and growth spurts. (You can put almost everything down to growth spurts. They're very handy that way.)

You're Not Tired

The single biggest mistake a new dad can make is to tell his partner that he's tired. Here is how that pans out. Him: 'I must be the tiredest person in the whole world.' Her: 'Oh really??' Him: 'I withdraw that statement, based on the mad look in your eyes.' Her: 'Good idea.'

Don't even go there. She spent eighteen hours pushing out that child in the labour ward. You just rubbed her back and said, 'Push away like mad, Ciara, you're doing great work.' You also found the time to get to level 400 in Angry Birds. Telling her how tired you are will introduce you to a whole new kind of angry bird. If you need to talk fatigue, I suggest you join DWAAC (Dads Who Aren't Allowed Complain). We meet every Tuesday night in the local hall. Pop down and tell us about your sleep deprivation, if you are allowed out.

You're Not Too Old

I reckon every man is too old to become a father. (I was forty-five when our eldest was born.)

The only males who have the energy to chase around after a toddler are nine-year-old boys. And society takes a fairly dim view of fathering a child before you get into your teens. (Unless you want to get on Jeremy Kyle. Although he probably wouldn't be interested unless you had that child with your cousin.)

So, don't worry that you waited until your late thirties or forties or whatever to have a crack at fatherhood. It's not like you were any better prepared for it in your early twenties. Unless the best way to prepare for fatherhood is drinking all weekend and a kebab addiction. Which it isn't.

Your House Is Too Small

The First Law of Having a Child: the amount of stuff you accumulate can and will spread to fill any space. I have carried out a quick, shoddy investigation into this and can now exclusively reveal the main culprit – seats. The average baby is the owner of three bouncy chairs, 1.3 buggies, four different types of booster chair and at least two car seats. That's a lot of seats for a tiny person with only one arse. There doesn't seem to be anything you can do about this. Except maybe reserve a skip now and see if they'll give you an early booking discount.

And Your Floor Isn't Suitable

Is there anything cooler than an old house with its original floorboards? Yes. Not spending three hours a day trying to prise bits of discarded baby rice out from between those boards would be great for starters. As for trying to pick up bits of broccoli thrown over the side of the high-chair … well, that depends on whether you want your baby to hear you using the f-word after every meal. (You're almost certainly looking at the c-word when it comes to old porridge.)

Here's my advice if you have gorgeous old floorboards in the dining room: laminate them. Unless you want Junior to be the first kid ever to be suspended from crèche for calling someone a you-know-what. Which isn't a great ambition for your child.

You're Too Tall

Forget about the sleepless nights. They're a cake-walk compared to the real test that lies ahead. That test would be the bending down. Let's face it – the last time you bent down was to pick up Hoggy when he fell flat on his face during your stag do in Budapest.

That's all about to change. For at least the first year of her life, your daughter is going to do all her best work in an area between zero and 10cm from the floor. If you think getting down there twenty-three times a day should be easy, wait until you try to get back up. Welcome to your glutes. I never thought I'd be going around recommending this, but you need to take up yoga.

You Have Fat Fingers

There is one certainty about fatherhood – your hands are too big. It's ironic really, because your chunky man-hands could well have been a major plus point in attracting a partner.

Now, those hands are your downfall. You'll only really appreciate it when it's time to change that first nappy in the hospital. This is your moment, where you show the world that you plan to be a hands-on father. Except you can't get your shovelly fist down the sleeve of the onesie, to ease in Sophie's tiny little arm. (They never show this in idyllic nappy ads, where it's all smiley young dads, with their American teeth.)

And when you eventually jiggle the poor child into the onesie, you can't get the shagging fasteners to close. This is usually where Jack or Sophie gets to hear their first curse. And their second and third. Worse again, your mother-in-law is probably there in the maternity ward to witness your foul-mouthed, big-handed cock-up. 'Jesus, Pat, I never knew you had such a short temper,' says she, not helping one bit.

You Will Be Jealous

Having young kids can turn you into a pitiless Green-Eyed Envy Monster. You watch a report on people displaced by floods in Slovakia and think, 'At least some of them might get a full night's sleep.' Or you pass some poor alcoholic drinking on the street and think, 'Isn't it well for some, cracking open the vino before lunch?' The worst of all? A friend says she got a hankering for a McDonald's, so she went out and got one. Just like that. She went out the door. The bitch.

You Need to Watch the Drink

It was traditional in the past for a father to take one look at his new child and retire to the pub for a minimum of three days. Great times. Unfortunately, you are now expected to help your partner during the first few days of your child's life. This usually involves buying eight packs of the wrong kind of nappy in the supermarket. You will get in so much trouble for that.

There is only one thing that could make this worse. A hangover. So, try to keep it to two bottles of beer when you get home from the maternity ward after the birth. Trust me, that's still going to seem like some kind of mad party compared to what lies ahead in the next six months.

You're Not Alone

Here's another thing worth doing while drinking your two bottles of post-maternity ward beer. Take a selfie of yourself relaxing on the sofa, alone in the house. It will be the last bit of time you will have to your selfie for the foreseeable future. Trust me, the slightest hint that you have nothing to do will get you a list of jobs faster than you can say, 'But I washed the bottles yesterday!' Your partner will not understand that we men are wired to sit and do nothing for hours on end, so that we can recover from chasing wild animals and that. Or maybe we're just lazy.

You Don't Know How to Dress Girls

Sorry guys, you don't. The problem is a lot of newborns seem to release a hormone in Dad that convinces him he is some kind of fashion guru. 'Why should it only be Mom who knows a good outfit?' says you, matching a stripy green top with pink tights. The result is a lot of little girls who look like they are coming from a fancy-dress party, where everyone went as Lady Gaga crossed with a clown.

Your partner's reaction will be, 'Jesus, what did Daddy dress you in, you poor child?' (This is how couples criticise each other, by talking through their child. My favourite one is, 'Will Mommy ever hurry on?')

My advice is to force your partner to always leave out clothes for your daughter by dressing the poor girl incredibly badly the first time you get the job. You should find this comes naturally.

You're Done with Foreign Holidays for a While

Going abroad with an eighteen-month-old is about as relaxing as taking a double dose of laxatives before heading in to sit a Leaving Cert Irish exam. Remember that forty-seven-year-old guy sitting on the plane with his child the last time you went on holidays? Well, he was only forty-two when he arrived at the check-in desk, two hours earlier. That's what trying to get an eighteen-month-old through an airport can do to a man. By the time he gets back from holidays, that guy will look old enough to retire. It's never worth it. Try a staycation until they are over two. (There are some days in Ireland when it actually doesn't rain.)

You're Not Hot

The good news is that you will get a fair bit of attention from hot women when you are out walking the baby. The bad news is that none of them are looking to start an affair with a sleep-deprived guy who hasn't managed to find time for a shower in three days. A lot of guys don't appreciate this. If you find yourself waving your little girl at a woman in Tesco and shouting, 'Look, look, she has my eyes', then you are probably one of them.

My guess is that a genuine Yummy Mummy spends as little time as possible with her own kids. She isn't going to be interested in yours. That said, there are plenty of places where you can meet women who like their kids. The swings at the playground are a particular favourite. As long as you don't turn to the hot mom pushing her kid next to you and say, 'Do you like swinging?' There's a thin line between harmless flirting and Dirty Dad. You'll have crossed it with that question.

You Need to Do Your Sums

The most important thing that a newbie dad should know? There will be a 'Time Away from the Child' meeting every Sunday night. This is where your partner tots up the time you spent away from the baby that week, compares it to the time she spent away from the baby and concludes that she is entitled to a fortnight in a 5-star spa retreat. That's tricky, and not just because you'll need a second mortgage to pay for it. Your problem is they don't allow kids in these 5-star resorts. Welcome to the longest fortnight of your life.

You Love Breastfeeding

Breastfeeding is a tricky business for dads. Don't worry about feeling useless during the first few months. At least you'll be asleep. The problem comes at weaning time. Or, as moms like to call it, 'All Yours'. You are handed a hungry, angry little man, who is basically a stranger because he has been latched on to mom for six months. The odds of him taking a bottle from you are about the same as the odds that he will suddenly start speaking Portuguese. As for the chances that his first words will be, 'Just drink the fucking bottle!' – they're pretty high.

You'll Fear the Playground

Some advice for when you bring your kid to the playground – beware the swings. You are there until your child decides otherwise. That means you are stuck talking to the parent pushing next to you, with no chance of escape. That's not so bad if she's a Yummy Mummy, but as I said above, you'll probably make a fool of yourself because you haven't had sex or sleep for three months. The problem arises when you get stuck with a parent who hasn't talked to another adult in two weeks. It's nearly always a new dad who has become obsessed with poo. And it's fair to say he's full of it.

You're a Big Eejit

This one is aimed at the moms out there. It isn't easy being a dad. The kids want us to behave like a cross between Homer Simpson and Dougal from *Father Ted*. We love that, it's like being back at college. Unfortunately, you moms expect us to switch into adult mode when the kids aren't around. The truth is we find the transition a bit tricky at times. Is there any chance we could have a thirty-minute No Fault window after the kids go to bed? If you could find a way to overlook the fact that we repeat everything you say in a stupid accent and call you Marge during that time, it would be great. Thanks in advance, Marge.

You Are Easily Distracted

Women get a mental upgrade when they give birth, which

gives them an internal project manager. Men? Not so much. One minute you are on your way to get a fresh pack of nappies out of the press. The next minute you are outside, painting the shed. You try to remember what triggered this change of tack; before you know it, you are cutting the grass. At this point her indoors comes outdoors and asks why she never got her nappies? And what's the story with the half-painted shed? Anyway, that's enough about distraction. Any man who started reading this paragraph has already gone off to empty the dishwasher.

You're Heading for Heartbreak

This is what happens when you have a girl. At some point between the age of two and three, your daughter will turn around and say the worst words any dad can hear (other than 'I have poos and it's too late'). Those words are 'Get away, Daddy.' All those years of being rejected by females won't help you prepare for this. The best reaction is to pretend to cry in a comical fashion (see 'You're a Big Eejit' above). The worst reaction is the genuine one, where you say, 'Nobody loves me' and burst into tears. Nobody wants Daddy to be that in touch with his feelings. Least of all you.

You're Taking the Clio

Most men have the same response when their partner announces a pregnancy. 'Fantastic news, we'll need a new car.' That's the good news. The bad news is, the new car isn't for you. Within six months it will belong to your partner. (She will mark her territory by putting one of her make-up bags in the driver-side door pocket.)

All the safety benefits you used to promote the idea of a new car, will now be used against you. 'I'm not risking my kids in that old banger,' says she, taking off in your brand-new Hyundai 4x4. And you're left driving around in a fifteen-year-old Clio. It's as humiliating as it sounds. This is the thin end of the wedge when it comes to car issues with kids; there's plenty more which you'll read about later on in the book.

You Need a Beard

It's a great way to swing some Me Time. A normal barber trip gets you about thirty minutes out of the house. This can't compete with the three hours your wife manages to squeeze out of a visit to the hairdressers. Any complaints will be put down with, 'You didn't have to push a baby out.' (Unless you did, in which case well done you.)

A beard is the perfect way to buy more time. Here is how it works. 1: Grow a beard. 2: Tell your wife it takes four hours to get it trimmed because she has no experience of maintaining a beard. (Unless she does, in which case I'm sorry for your troubles.) 3: Go to a barber that does decent beard trims. It will be packed with beardy dads, so you'll have to queue for ages. 4: Read a seven-year-old copy of *Golf Digest*. You'd be surprised how enjoyable that can be when you don't have a toddler trying to torture you into giving him another rice cake. 5: Sit back and let a jovial Turkish gentleman pamper you for half an hour. It is actually better than sex. 6: Don't say this to your partner.

You're a Bad Listener. Got it?

Here is the essence of New Dad in two simple steps. 1: Your partner tells you to do three things. 2: You forget one of them. Some scientists argue that new fathers are programmed to ignore their partners so they can listen out for wild animals approaching the cave. Those scientists are probably New Dads, desperately looking for an out.

We all know the real reason is that there was a piece on the radio about Cristiano Ronaldo moving back to Man United, at the same time you were being told the thing that you promptly forgot. (It was to put a new packet of wipes on the changing table, by the way. It always is.)

I wouldn't admit the Ronaldo to United excuse unless you fancy a move of your own, to the spare room, with the baby. The real problem here is that a lot of men show signs of being a good listener before the first baby arrives and scrambles their brain. That leaves you defenceless when you can't remember the direct order about the wipes.

There is a simple solution. Once the pregnancy test gives a positive, you need to stop listening. With any luck, your partner will accept over time that you are just a bad listener and will focus on your positive attributes. If your listening skills are what she likes most about you, then I would say it's game over.

You're Not Owed a Thing

Remember those Friday nights you babysat your brother's kids, in the hope that what goes around comes around? Bad news. There is no Karma in babysitting. All that happened is your brother remembered he has a social life. He is about as likely to give up a Friday night to mind your kids as he is to watch *Bridget Jones' Diary* while eating a tub of ice cream.

The result? Now that you have kids, your Friday night revolves around Graham Norton and frozen pizza. The moral? Never babysit during your child-free years. In fact, never stay in during your child-free years. Get out there while you can.

You Won't Believe the Cost of Childcare

They say the Scandinavians are cool and calm characters who don't get phased by anything. Well, you should have seen the look on their faces when I told them the cost of childcare in Ireland.

The latest figures suggest you can expect to pay between €1,000 and €1,500 a month for a full-time place in a private crèche. The government allows two years of free pre-school from the age of three; but that only gives you three hours a day, with two months off during summertime.

An early childcare subsidy, introduced in 2017 for kids up to the age of three, will give back €1,000 a year to most parents with kids in full-time care. (The subsidy rises for parents on lower incomes.) But given the annual cost is still up around the €15,000 mark per child, that's an awful lot of people paying an awful lot of money.

You might be able to persuade your own parents to take up the slack. (29% of respondents in a recent survey said they use relatives for childcare.) It can be hard to get retired parents to mind your kids now, though, because they seem to spend most of the year in Lanzarote. (Particularly after a grandchild is born, I think you'll find.)

Be careful if you are selecting an au pair. Your partner might be feeling a bit body conscious after giving birth. (Luckily the *Daily Mail* is there to help boost her confidence with photos of celebrity moms in bikinis.) You don't want to be looking at the profiles of candidates on an au pair site and insisting she should at least interview that Spanish girl who looks like a cross between Penelope Cruz and Sofia Vergara. I actually heard of one mother who was so riddled with jealousy that she drove her au pair to the airport with a one-way ticket back to Madrid.

Worse again, I've heard from some dads that their au pairs don't give them the time of day. You'd think they'd give poor Dad the odd look, for all the jealousy and trouble they cause. (I'm messing. For any au pair reading this, please don't give Dad the eye. He'll just go out and buy skinny jeans and a pair of designer skate-boarding shoes, and it will all turn very messy.)

You Will Eat Junk

You probably thought you'd spend the hour after the kids go to bed chatting through the events of the day with your partner. But it's impossible to talk when you have two Yorkies and half a tube of Pringles in your mouth at the same time. Kids. They turn you into a junk junkie.

You're in Luck

This is the only bit that really matters. All being well, at some point just after the birth the midwife will hand you the baby swaddled in blankets, so you can look after her for a minute. You think you're going to be prepared for this, but you won't be. It will feel like your head is going to blow off with the euphoria. This is the only real job you've had all day, other than not getting upset when your partner goes ballistic after you brought a sharing pack of Doritos into the delivery ward. So, breathe slowly for sixty seconds and take in the best thing that ever happened in your life. And don't drop her.

That Said …

It's tough. Having kids is tough. Freeze frame the magic minutes in your brain, because there are times when you will need them. A friend of mine recommended mindfulness as a way to live in the now and appreciate the good times when they are happening. I was too tired to read the mindfulness books, so I just made a point of reminding myself every now and again to stop and watch the kids, forget about everything else. I recommend you try something similar. Because the arrival of a new child will knock the stuffing out of you, making it hard to enjoy the moment. I should have warned you earlier, but I was afraid I'd put you off and you'd carry on enjoying your childless life, which is making me mad jealous.

You have no idea how annoying it was listening to you banging on about your amazing city break in Antwerp. Particularly since we were just back from a weekend in Peppa Pig World ourselves. They play the Peppa theme tune there, all the time. You don't even know what I'm talking about, because you don't have kids. I'm on the verge of tears just thinking about it.

Enough of the foolishness. Hopefully this has given you a flavour of what happens to you and your life when baby arrives. If it seems a bit downbeat and negative, then that's deliberate, because I felt it was important to counter the 'kids are life-changing' crowd, who seem to think it's all sweetness and light. (Or maybe they are away a lot on business and someone else is raising their kids. You can't rule that out.)

But I've honestly experienced more joy in the first five years of fatherhood than I did in the forty-five years that came before it. That's the thing about being a dad. Life gets tough and amazing at the same time. Here are some of the things I enjoy the most.

1.2 THE BEST DAYS OF YOUR LIFE

Release the Eejit

As I said earlier, men are basically eejits. We have to hide this in adult life or else no one would sleep with us or give us a mortgage. But inside every one of us, there's a ten-year-old boy giggling at a joke he heard about a Chinese dentist. And then your first child comes along. Not only are you allowed to release your inner eejit, it's actually your job as chief entertainer to act the eejit. All of a sudden, it's okay to run around in public singing, 'The first mate's name was Carter, by Christ he was a farter.' It's great to have that kind of song back in your life again. Just make sure you have the kids with you when you decide to give it a blast in public. Otherwise, it's a really bad look. (Unless you're with a bunch of blokes, in which case knock yourself out.)

You're Hilarious

Small kids will laugh at anything. And given that you are Chief Eejit, they will spend most of their time laughing at you. It's good to know you still have it on the sense of humour front. Just don't get carried away and tell your partner you are thinking of putting that on your Tinder profile. That's not funny to someone who hasn't slept in a fortnight. You'll just end up trying to make your kids laugh, every second weekend, at a McDonald's halfway between their home and your mange-ridden bedsit.

What I would say is this; there are times when your kids will come up and demand your attention. You might want to shoo them away because you need some space or you're wrecked. Before doing that, try this. Make a funny face and a dinosaur sound. Look at their faces. Maybe you don't feel that tired any more.

Sorry Old Man

It's the middle of the night. Your three-year-old wakes for the fifth time because her toy fish, Nemo, has gone missing in the bed. (It's her version of *Finding Nemo*. Never show them a movie.) And then it occurs to you. Your dad went through all this with you and never said a word. You think about calling him up to say sorry for all the mockery and self-righteous arrogance you put his way during your teenage years; you might even go all in and tell him that you love him. You decide against it because it's four in the morning; he'll probably think you opened the second bottle of wine, and you with small kids to mind. From then on, you see your own dad in a new light. Not that you'll ever tell him. Sure, it would only go to his head.

Seriously though, having kids of your own is a great way to reconnect with your parents. Particularly if they're not too old and could be tapped up for a spot of childminding.

Stretches

All those guys out doing Tough Mudder and Extreme Marathons to try to hide the fact they're forty-five? Total waste of money. There is no better full body workout on the market right now than looking after a child up to the age of six. Your ageing muscles will thank you for clearing up two bags of Mega Bloks, four times a day.

Fancy taking up white-collar boxing? No need, just have a little boy and he'll beat the living crap out of you for free.

As for walking up and down the stairs seventy-three times a day because you keep forgetting stuff? Congratulations. That's quite a low number for someone trying to survive on eight minutes of sleep.

I'm not suggesting this is enough exercise. Kids will make sure you don't slouch around on the couch; it's up to you to supplement this with regular exercise outside the house once or twice a week. You're not just tuning up your body with that. You need to get the endorphins flowing, away from the kids.

I play squash and go African Drumming once a week. (On separate nights – it's almost impossible to dig a shot out of the back corner while playing a samba beat.) Those hobbies work for me, because I'm letting other people down if I shy out of them. If you haven't got one or two things like that in your life, I recommend you go find them. You need an out.

Career

People think that having a child can put a halt on your career. That's wrong for two reasons. The first one is the one you share with everyone. 'I have to do well at work now that I have kids,' says you. Go on, you big hairy caveman, providing for your family.

The second reason? 'I need to earn more than my partner. Otherwise it will make financial sense for me to give up my job and mind the kids. There is no way I'm getting stuck at home with those crazies, clearing up Mega Bloks every hour and trying not to watch *Judge Judy*.' You keep this to yourself because you're a modern man and all that. But it's kind of true nonetheless.

Joking aside, I think having kids will make you more focused on your career. This isn't just so you can make more money, although that is part of it. This focus is also a stage of life thing; now that the kids are here, you start planning ahead in decades rather than weeks. I certainly took stock when the kids arrived. I take half a day a week off to mind them while my wife is at work and I still get more done every week than I did before.

New Skills

You'll need to pick up no end of new skills with kids in the house. Eating a Yorkie in one go in case one of the crazies walks into the room is impressive enough. But actually talking to them with the Yorkie still in your mouth when they burst into the room – that should have its own category on *Britain's Got Talent*.

As for using the world's smallest screwdriver to open the battery compartment of a toy while a child screams 'It stopped working' directly into your ear – you'll pick that up in no time. Because the alternative isn't worth it.

I always saw myself as a DIY disaster before the kids arrived. My wife still does, but that's a bit unfair considering I put together a flat-pack chest of drawers and half a Little Tikes house, both of which are still standing.

Other things I'm getting good at include wiping other people's bums, taking out a hair-tie without making my daughter cry and persuading her brother to come in for his dinner without threatening to burn all his toys. Society doesn't put a huge value on these things, but trust me, they are some of the most important things I'll ever do.

Talking Points

There is a notion out there that all men like talking about sports. We don't. It's just that we have nothing else in common. And then kids come along. All of a sudden, you're pushing a conversation point along in a buggy. Who wants to talk about José Mourinho to a strange man when you can swap stories about head lice? You'll even find you have something to say to strange women other than, 'I think your dress would look better on my bedroom floor.' (Stay classy.)

I wasn't expecting this. The stereotype maintains that men aren't that interested in their kids, at least compared to football, cycling and politics. This couldn't be more wrong. Whenever I'm having a pint or a coffee with guys who have young kids, we get the superfluous stuff out of the way first, before moving on to the big issue. And that big issue is the kids who have changed everything. It's the only thing we really want to talk about. Who knew?

The Leaves

But really, the best thing about being a dad is that you start to notice the leaves again. Or at least you notice your little girl walking down the footpath kicking her way through the autumn leaves and remember that you used to do that too, a million years ago, when you were the little one.

The general idea is you are supposed to lead your kids through life. The reality is that your kids are out in front, showing you the magic in all the simple things that got lost over the years. And then their toy breaks and it's your job to fix it. But it's well worth it.

1.3 THE MOTHERHOOD EFFECT

Maybe it's just me, but it felt like we only really became adults when the kids came along. My wife made the transition the minute she got pregnant, planning five years ahead and stuff like that. I followed her into adulthood shortly after, because it was clear she didn't want to stay married to a man-child.

I'm a different person to the man I was five years ago, when my daughter was born; I talk about these changes right across this book. But the changes to your partner are vital too, as they have a huge impact on your relationship. Here are the big changes I reckon motherhood brings to a woman, so you are aware of the pitfalls before you walk into one of them. (These changes aren't all based on my wife, just the good ones.)

Germ Warfare

You will be sent on a shopping expedition soon after the baby is brought home from hospital. You will arrive back with a kitchen cleaner that kills 99.99% of all known germs. You will be told that you are putting your child at the mercy of .01% of all known germs. You will be sent back to the shop.

A new baby in the house means that Mom is engaged in a fight to the death with an army of invisible germs. You are either on board with that or else you are basically on the side of the germs. So, don't make a smart comment about the packs of anti-bacterial wipes spread throughout the house. Or else you could be compared to those people who appeased Hitler in the run-up to the Second World War.

In fact, I'd strongly recommend you carry some Milton spray with you at all times around the house, just to show that you are up for the fight. One thing worth noting: this germ warfare is a first baby thing. The second child could be licking the cat's arse before you get sent off to find some antiseptic wipes. Don't worry – you'll still have about twenty packets of them at the back of the press.

Shopping

The arrival of a child in the house brings out the strongest female instinct of them all – shopping. You will be familiar with her pre-pregnancy shopping. That's where she bought a new top every weekend, just because she could. Motherhood changes all that. She will lay off buying any new tops until she reaches her post-baby target weight. If you think that means she will cut out shopping for a year, then you've obviously never met a baby who owns 537 onesies.

It can be hard for Mom to get out the door with a new-born baby. But not as hard as trying to get back in the door, carrying two bags from Baby Zara and one each from Gap, Penneys and H&M. And it will sometimes feel like her new catchphrase is, 'There's more in the car.'

Don't make a smartarse comment like, 'Tell me again why he needs fourteen hats.' That is easily countered with, 'Tell you what – next time you can come shopping with me.' Yikes.

Remember that any reduction in baby-shopping will mean a rise in shopping for herself. And you'll be back in that changing room with your partner, saying all the wrong things when asked, 'Are these jeans a bit too young for me?'

The Mammy Factor

We all like to think we are different to our parents. That's easy when you are single – just never refer to the slightly later sunsets in early March as a 'grand stretch'. But then baby comes along. And your partner becomes Mammy.

This is tough for women. They see themselves as Mom rather than Mammy. There is a huge difference. Mammy was a frazzled woman in comfortable shoes, who was lucky if she got out once a month. Mom wears Converse runners and has three brunches a day with other Moms, also in Converse runners. All the Moms have fabulous hair. That's the dream.

The reality is that only two of the Moms could make it. And they have a fair bit of puke in their hair.

The first sign that Mom is in fact Mammy is in the use of religious language. Never mind that your partner is a committed atheist. Two weeks with a new baby and she'll be saying things like 'God protect us' and 'You'd want the patience of Job'. (Job was very patient, by all accounts.)

The other sign of Mammy is food. Mom swears she will feed her little girl polenta and line-caught tuna. Mammy gives that up after a few days and starts shovelling bacon and cabbage into little Sophie. Sure it didn't do us any harm, says she, every inch her mother.

Packing

Forget about baby brain. Women have a super-computer installed at the moment they give birth. Why? Because nothing else will do when it comes to calculating all the things that could happen when they leave the house with a new baby. You probably think it's okay to just swan out the door with two nappies, a packet of wipes and a spare onesie. That's a typical man of course, gambling that you won't get stuck in a snowstorm. In Ireland. In July.

Take a look inside your partner's changing bag the next time she goes to visit her mother. There is an entire change of outfit in case the baby explodes out of all ends. There is also a change of clothes in the next size up, in case the baby goes through a sudden growth spurt. (You can't be too careful.) And there are four different meals in case they get stranded by flash floods.

The main problem with your partner's super-computer is you didn't get one. So you'll end up facing some awkward 'did you remember to bring' questions, as you walk out the door. Lie with an 'Of course I did' and head for the car, hoping you have covered every eventuality. Don't worry – it's pretty unlikely that you will get attacked by that gang of vicious swans.

Decision Maker

A new mom is good at making decisions. This can come as a surprise, because pre-baby women can be slow to make up their minds. If you doubt this, just watch two women trying to pick a place to meet. 'Whatever suits you.' 'I don't mind.' 'I really don't mind.' 'I really, really don't mind.' 'How about Such and Such?' 'I hate that place.' 'I thought you didn't mind?'

Suddenly baby comes along and it's one fast decision after another. The baby will be breastfed, weaned onto broccoli and sent to a Gaelscoil because she thinks there are too many hippies at the Educate Together. You might have been consulted when these decisions were being made, but you were probably trying to read something on your phone.

A word of warning. You will sometimes feel a strange urge to get involved in parenting your kids. This might involve saying something like, 'My friend Gerry at work says his wife thinks that your baby-led weaning is a big mistake.' Let us know how you get on with that one. From your new bedroom in the garden shed.

1.4 DADDY LANDMINES

You're not really supposed to say this any more, but men are in fact different to women. This will only become more apparent when you have kids together. The problem is that any small difference in world view can result in things going a bit nuclear after seven months without sleep.

Here are some of the key areas of difference you need to keep an eye on, to make sure that your marriage is kiddie-proof.

Nesting

Some definitions will help here. **Nesting**: The process where a pregnant woman with impeccable taste takes a chic, modern home and tries to turn it into a doll's house. **Pointless**: Any attempt to stop her. **Aaaaw**: What you must say when it's finished. **Do you not think it's a bit *My Big Fat Gypsy Wedding*?**: What you must not say when it's finished. (Are you nuts?) **Weird**: The urge you get to buy a €5,000 TV and sound system just because your partner is doing the place up. **Unprintable**: What your partner says to that idea.

Clothes

Men are outsiders when it comes to the whole 'clothing the child' thing. It starts when you wander into the nursery one day and notice a chest of drawers full of baby clothes. Where did they come from, you say to yourself and not your partner, because that means a long chat on taking responsibility for your child and that never ends well. (It doesn't even start well.)

The day will come when you will be allowed to dress the

child for an outing. You'll get it completely wrong. An in-house review (your partner) will conclude you were trying to either freeze or roast your own child. There is nothing you can do about this.

Then there is the small matter of putting a red cardigan over a pink top. The problem there is that you think it is a small matter.

Here is another landmine. You squeeze your daughter into a onesie, even though it is clearly too small. You don't ask your partner about this. That is because you are only allowed to ask five questions a day about child-rearing, after which you have to figure it out yourself. (Nightmare.) Later, your partner asks why you used a onesie that is clearly too small. You respond by asking what that onesie was doing in the drawer, when it should have been in storage. Two hours later you move back in with your mother. Seriously, we've lost some of our best men to that one. So steer clear of the smart remarks. Remember, we're all tired and snappy.

Organisation

Your partner is programmed to detect the slightest change in your new baby. Hence the four words that a man is most likely to hear when there is a new baby in the house – 'Get me the thermometer.' Naturally, you have no idea where the thermometer is. Unfortunately, you have already used up your daily ration of five child-related questions. So now you are heading into the unknown.

You check the medicine box. There was a time when that consisted of two packets of Nurofen Plus and some Alka-

Seltzer from 2007. Now that baby is here, it carries the stock levels of a medium-sized pharmacy. What it doesn't carry is the thermometer. (Or at least it doesn't carry the latest thermometer. You'll find that Mom likes to stock a wide variety of temperature-taking thingies, so she can double-check her results.) You vaguely remember being handed that thermometer the last time and being told to put it back in the medicine box. If you can remember it, she can definitely remember it. Pressure.

There is only one place you can think of – the drawer below the cutlery drawer in the kitchen. That's your go-to miscellaneous spot, where you put stuff that you were told to put away but can't remember where it belongs. You open the drawer and there it is, along with those two missing sippy cups that got you in so much trouble last week. Just then word comes through from the bedroom that the baby is staging one of his trademark recoveries. You put the thermometer back in the medicine box. Phew. And so ends the latest episode, up there with *The Bourne Identity* on the nerve-racking front.

Education

Six centimetres. That is how much your partner is dilated in the delivery room when she starts to think about schools. It's around the same time you start to wonder if there is any chance of popping out for a bag of chips. (There isn't. Okay? There isn't.)

Over the next few months she will consider moving house, becoming a Quaker or even learning Irish in the hope of getting Sophie and Jack into a good school. You won't do any of these things. That's because there are forms of pond life where the male of the species does more planning than Mad Dad, when it comes to education.

You have only one thing on your mind when it comes to your kids' education. Traffic. So, while herself is checking online forums for views on various schools, you are all over Google Maps to make sure you can make the morning drop without getting caught in gridlock. Your focus is so pure, you can watch a television exposé on drug use in a particular school and still admire the fact that is perfectly located for the M50. It's admirable, in a way.

You will of course go along to meet the principals of various schools. At the 'any other questions' bit at the end, you'll pipe up with your carefully prepared questions on rush-hour traffic in the area. Here's the thing. If the principal is a man, he'll be happy to talk about that for hours. In fact, it might be just the thing to get Jack into that school. And they said you were useless when it came to kids and education!

Tidiness

Planning for kids? You need to find a partner who's messier than you. Here's why. There's a Messiness Index (MI) that goes from one to ten. Ten is tidy, one is your sock drawer. Research (mine) shows that a woman's MI score rises by two for every child. Basically, she gets tidier in response to a growing family. Your best bet is to find a woman that is messier than you at the outset; at least then you have a buffer when she starts to rise up the MI charts. This is vital unless you enjoy the phrase, 'How many times do I have to tell you?'

Bear in mind that your partner's MI score will rise temporarily when you are expecting visitors. It goes up one for her relations, two for yours and three when the public-health nurse is due for the six-week visit. (Public health nurses are very judgemental, apparently.)

Here is a fail-safe way to test your potential partner's MI score. Hang your coat on the back of a kitchen chair. If her reaction is to go ballistic, it's never going to work. If, on the other hand, she waltzes into the dining room and puts her coat over yours on the back of the chair, you're probably looking at 'the one'. You might want to marry her, or renew your vows or something – that kind of woman is in demand.

Weaning

The process of getting a baby off milk and on to solids. As if you didn't know that (after googling it in a panic one day when herself asked if you had any plans for the weaning process). It turns out you have the sum total of one plan for the weaning process. And that is to avoid it.

It also turns out that this is a mistake. Here's the thing. There are two roles when it comes to weaning – preparing the food and cleaning up afterwards. If you think the preparation bit is a nightmare, then you have never tried to clean up after a six-month-old has gone toe-to-toe with a bowl of steamed broccoli. Here's my advice – steal a march on this one and say you want to be in charge of preparing the purée. Maybe suggest this when your partner is really tired and less likely to say, 'Hang on a minute, the only bit of child-rearing you've done so far is look up schools on Google Maps – what's your game?'

If you get the nod, steam and mash forty-seven sweet potatoes and a bag of apples. That's you done except for the feeding. You can save time for the first month by just spooning the mush straight onto the bib, rather than running it briefly through the child. Best of luck!

1.5 WHAT KIND OF DAD DO YOU WANT TO BE?

As I said at the outset, this book is mainly about my experiences of fatherhood. There is every chance you are not like me and will have a completely different reaction to a kid around the place. I'd like to say that this is a good thing and diversity makes the world a better place; but secretly, I'll be judging you for not doing things the way I do them. (Judging other people's parenting decisions is one of the best things about having kids. Sometimes, it's the only thing that keeps me going.)

Here are some of the types of other dads I've noticed. Which one of them are you?

Always Busy Dad (ABD)

If you're looking for ABD, try the kitchen sink. That's where he likes to spend three hours a day, washing the same two cups while listening to the radio. This is no accident. ABD surveyed the situation when the kids arrived and quickly realised that the devil makes work for idle hands. He doesn't say that phrase out loud any more, because it's a long way back when you refer to your partner as the devil. His favourite phrase? 'You wouldn't say that if you'd spent half the morning struggling with a stubborn tea stain.' His least favourite phrase? 'Just put it in the dishwasher, Always Busy Dad, I need a hand with the kids in the front room.'

Overly Proud Dad (OPD)

He's the one with the baby-carrying sling. OPD is so keen to show that he's a father that he likes to wear the sling around town even when he doesn't have little Jack with him. Or at least he did, until a woman pointed at him and roared, 'That fool is after forgetting his child somewhere.' He now realises how a childless sling might be a bad look for him.

OPD loves the fact that Yummy Mummies approach him in the supermarket when he has little Jack in the sling. His favourite phrase? 'Don't ever grow up Jack – I don't think I can live without the attention.' His least favourite phrase? 'I want to get out and walk Dad, I'm nearly five years of age.'

Old-Fashioned Dad

He wasn't always old-fashioned, you know. OFD was a feminist in his day, just the man to stand up for equal rights in the pub if he thought it might land him a bit of sex. It did and that's how he ended up with a small child. And a strong notion that the woman's place is in the home. His favourite phrase? 'I must go away out and do a job, it could take anything up to a fortnight.' His least favourite phrase? 'I'll fix the lawnmower, Old-Fashioned Dad, you stay here and feed the kids.'

Daddy Pig Dad

DPD has been watching too much television. In particular, he's been watching too much *Peppa Pig* with the kids, when he should have been reading them a book. The result is that he is slowly morphing into Daddy Pig. He now speaks with a soft, posh English accent and tends to call his young fella George. He was being treated by a doctor for the condition, but had to move to another surgery after saying 'Hello, Miss Rabbit' to the lady at reception. His favourite phrase is two grunts followed by 'It turns out I'm the world champion at that.' His least favourite phrase? 'Daddy, I think we're watching too much television.'

Project Manager Dad

PMD successfully managed the transition to Version 7 of the software at work. Nothing could be harder than that, said he, opening a new spreadsheet to manage the rearing of his little daughter. The big eejit. He is currently at Version 7097 of the project plan, after the little tyke failed to count to six when she hit eighteen months. A recent meeting of 'all the stakeholders' was interrupted when his little girl sang a word-perfect verse of 'The Wheels on the Bus'. PMD said, 'I'd love to enjoy this moment, but you were supposed to do that last week.'

Party On Dad

POD isn't the type of man to let a few kids ruin his active social life. Your standard POD has only one question for the potential mother of his children. 'Would you have any problem with a stranger rearing our kids so we can go to Berlin for a week around Christmas time?' A 'no' there means he has found his perfect partner, Party On Mom (POM).

Another type of POD fails to find a POM and ends up

with a crazy woman who thinks they should bring the kids on holidays with them. This POD can be found at the kiddy disco on holidays, dad-dancing to 'Uptown Funk'. He's never going to let it go.

Very Foolish Dad

VFD likes to repeat half-arsed child-rearing advice he heard at work. 'John's wife had their young fella on solids by four months, you know,' says VFD, as his own wife googles 'affordable hitmen in your area'.

'How did she manage that?' asks his wife wearily, because she's been down this road before.

'I didn't bother asking him,' replies Very Foolish Dad, as herself messages a dodgy man called Jorge to check his availability. 'I just thought you should know how John's wife was getting on.'

'Thanks for all your help over the past year,' replies his wife.

'You'd swear you were saying goodbye to me or something,' replies VFD, right for once.

Overly Sentimental Dad

You know him all right. He's the guy blubbing away when his daughter hits one week old, because they grow up so quickly.

Six months later he's over the moon that her first words are Dada, but then immediately starts to miss the way she used to gurgle and point at things.

His favourite phrase? 'Her first steps will be her first steps away from me.'

And least favourite? 'I'm a big girl now, Daddy.'

1.6 TIME FOR A CHANGE OF CAR

It is a magical moment in any man's life. You sit with your arms around your partner, waiting for the indicator on the Clearblue pregnancy test to deliver its verdict. The result is positive. A whole range of emotions sweep through your brain. The main one being, I have a cast-iron excuse to spend a month on the Internet looking up people carriers. (Well, if she can do it for a buggy, why can't I do it for a car?)

Here's what I noticed on the car front, once the kids came along.

Which Car?

A message from your back and your glutes: that low-slung, sporty Honda you've been driving for the past five years has got to go. Yes, you've had great times together, driving around with your partner when neither of you had a care in the world. But it's like Honours Limbo Dancing, trying to get a baby seat in the tight and narrow back doors. Once in there, you might have to do some strap adjustment before driving off. You're tired and it's raining. Your back is telling you it's time to lie down for a month.

This would be much easier in a people carrier. Yes, those cars scream, 'I'm old, and no one will ever want to have sex with me again.' But not as loud as your three-month-old is screaming because you can't get her into the back of that low-slung, sporty Honda. So, do your back a favour and go for boring on the car front.

An MPV like a Renault Scenic or Opel Zafira is always good. The Hyundai ix35 says a bit about the owner. I have a sense of style. I have a few bob. My mother will be delighted because she'll think it's a Range Rover.

I don't know about your finances, but you'll probably be able to buy a new car with one of those PCP leasing deals. Ignore the fact the whole thing seems a bit dodgy and you should be banned from signing any form of loan application while surviving on no sleep for a week. Because if there is one thing we learned from the property crash here, it's that nothing can possibly go wrong when gangs of Irish people sign loan deals that seem too good to be true.

Which Car Seat?

You'll need a car seat to bring baby home. This involves sleeping in your car outside some place like Mothercare. That saves you the bother of driving up and down there eight times a day for 'another look'. Your strategy in the car-seat shop is simple. Nod at everything and don't tell the hot Lithuanian shop assistant she should try to make it as a model. You'd be amazed how badly that goes down with a seven-month pregnant partner. After thirty-three visits, the seat you looked at the first day will be chosen and strapped into the car. Just shake it twice and say, 'That seems fine to me.' Anything more and you'll be back in for another look. And not at the hot Lithuanian, before you ask.

By the way, you might notice that some families have two different brands of car seat in the back. Have two kids yourself and you'll soon figure it out. The first-born's first car seat is designed by a team of scientists lured from NASA. The seat is so tough that Conor McGregor refuses to fight it. It is made in Scandinavia, because Scandinavians are better than us. It costs more than the car.

But it's carrying a precious cargo, so who cares? Well, you do when the second baby arrives and you google 'childcare costs in Ireland'. That explains why, when it comes to buying a new, bigger seat for the first child, they usually end up in a brand called El Cheapo Seato. It might be made in Mexico using child labour for all you know. But it's only €150, so maybe better not to ask. The good news is it passes all the safety regulations. The bad news is it doesn't have any Scandinavian hipster credentials, but who can afford those any more?

Here's the bottom line. Go with El Cheapo Seato, for everyone, from day one. That way, all your kids will get a decent seat for a decent price.

Whose Car Is It Anyway?

There is a scene in *The Simpsons* where Nelson laughs at a man driving along in a car that is clearly too small for him. My guess is that man is a new dad. And he ended up with the banger. Here's how that works. Man has nice big car. Man and partner get pregnant. Woman gets nice new car. Man gets her old car. It's neither nice nor big. There is no water in the windscreen washer bottle.

You'll be lucky if you ever get a run in that new people carrier. Outside of the 'putting the baby to sleep' run (see below), there are only two situations where you will be allowed in the driver's seat. When Mom hasn't had time to put on her make-up before leaving the house, or when there is a bit of parallel parking to be done. (Come on, Moms, we all know it's true.)

Bear this in mind when you start your search for people carriers on the Internet. And make sure you have enough money left over to buy a decent car for yourself. Otherwise you'll just end up driving around in a 1998 Micra, wondering if you would have been better off getting a vasectomy. And there's bound to be a Nelson judging you from the side of the road.

Will I Ever Sleep Again?

Not until your youngest child hits two. That said, your child will be more inclined to sleep in a comfortable car. This matters more than you could imagine. When all else has failed (a bath, watching Baby Einstein videos, Calpol, Neoclarityn, a couple of books, cursing), you can always just put them in the car and go. It's also a great solution when your toddler starts to fight the midday nap. Some of the sweetest hours as a new dad are spent cruising along a motorway while your pride and joy is legally restrained in the back. In fact, any political party looking to appeal to new parents in Dublin should just offer to turn the M50 into a full circle. You could cruise around with your baby all day long.

But then the tide turns. You know this has happened to a couple when you see them in the car, jumping up and down and making faces at a two-year-old in the back. There is no need to call the police. This couple are just trying to stop their little darling from taking a late afternoon nap. Because 'little' and 'darling' are not the two words you would use to describe the child when he is still bouncing off the ceiling at 11 p.m. that night. (Actually, little is one of them. Darling isn't.)

1.7 HANDLING THE HOUSEWORK

Sorry to be the bearer of bad news, but parenting isn't really pushing baby around in a buggy for an hour, followed by a sneaky pint on the way home. It's mainly about three loads of washing a day and whose turn it is to clean up the mess in the front room. It's no surprise that housework is cited by many former couples as the reason their relationship didn't work.

Here's what I've learned in the last five years.

Step Away from the Washing Machine

The male brain cannot absorb the Rules of Washing Clothes. Some of our best men have been looking at it for years and we're still nowhere near a solution. Here's the low-down.

A minimum of three items that you put into a forty-degree wash should have gone into a wool wash, and now they're ruined, you stupid man. An item from Penneys can be put in any wash, it doesn't matter, sure I'll just get another one. And finally, the only way to find the missing towel you were told you had to put in the wash, is to turn the machine on. At this point the towel will make itself apparent to you, outside the washing machine, the door of which is now locked for 120 minutes. You are so dead. There are two solutions here. Buy an expensive new machine that will allow you to add items mid-wash. Or else throw the towel in the bin and say nothing. Option two is your friend here.

Make Space for the Cleaning Lady

Irish people are slow to hire a cleaning lady, in case their pass-remarkable cousin says, 'That one is up herself.' (Being 'up yourself' is the lowest of the low in Ireland, and I'd say it's quite painful.)

Anyway, this cleaning lady resistance lasts until a child arrives. Two weeks and 736 housework arguments later, it emerges that the hourly rate for a cleaner is 10% of the amount a solicitor will charge to manage your divorce. Enter the cleaning lady. However, this is Ireland, so this new cleaner must also become your friend. You will be like some kind of Mrs Doyle, badgering the poor lady with offers of cups of tea and apologising for the state of the jacks. ('I told him there was something off about that curry.') There are no winners here. So when the cleaner comes to do her job, give her a break and head out for a walk.

Handheld Is Your Friend

Just a quick word on handheld vacuum cleaners. Buy forty and scatter them around the house. They'll save your back from a load of bending down to pick up crumbs from the couch, and some of the more expensive models have enough suction to pick up a small child. That's all you need to know here.

Hug that Dishwasher

You need to embrace your inner housewife. Why? Because the alternative is playing with your kids. This isn't to suggest they're not lovely and all. But every second spent loading the dishwasher is another second not spent building a wooden railway so your two-year-old can smash it apart. That isn't even fun the first time.

Seasoned parents will often race their partner through

dinner to get the coveted dishwasher gig. The key is to spend ages reloading it, to fit in that final cup. This is often accompanied by the sounds of your partner screaming, 'Why did you ask me to build it for you so?' from another room. You and the dishwasher – these are the real golden moments.

You Like Gardening Now?

You'll find a lot of new dads banging on about their geraniums. This has less to do with a love of gardening and more to do with the fact that you can shout, 'Keep away from me, I'm going to turn on the strimmer' at your pesky kids. It's basically the outdoors, Me-Time version of loading the dishwasher. Which is why it doesn't count. I checked with the authorities in this area (my wife), and apparently any outdoors work doesn't count as housework. So, cut the hedge all you like. But there's a pile of laundry to be folded when you come in. Just so you know.

Avoid the Socks

Speaking of laundry, not all washing loads are equal. As in, some have two sheets and a pair of jeans, while others have small people's socks. This matters when you are hanging them out. Let's just say a laundry basket of kids' undies is enough to make you wish you'd joined the priesthood. (It's that bad.)

I did the sums recently while hanging out such a wash. My kids clearly have four arses and eight legs each. Here's the lowdown. The kids' sock-wash line-hang is two hours of your life down the tubes. So try to hand it over to someone else.

Mammy Likes a Remark

You know how it goes. Your mother calls over to pawn off some pork chops that are out of date tomorrow. 'Sure, just throw them in the bin if you don't want them.' As if you don't have enough to do. You are folding the laundry when she calls.

'I see she has you well trained.'

'What's that supposed to mean, Mammy?'

'Just that you never did that when you were living in my house.'

'You wouldn't let me.'

'I would if you'd offered. I'm delighted to see you're willing to do it for someone else. Even if you're folding those T-shirts the wrong way.'

'Is it possible for you to sit there without passing comment?'

'Not really. And that's no way to talk to someone who just brought you some lovely pork chops. They're in date and everything.'

The take-away here: don't do housework in front of your mother. It never ends well.

They're Not Helping

The sentence that a toddler hears the most? 'You're old enough now to clean up your own mess.' Actually, that's not entirely true. Those are the words spoken by her dad, on the verge of tears because the front room looks like a bomb wouldn't need to hit it.

Based on extensive research, I can now reveal what the toddler actually hears. 'Please put one piece of your jigsaw puzzle back in the box before wandering off to dress the cat as a pirate.' In fairness, I was a messy child, so my daughter didn't exactly pick it up off the floor. The problem is, she doesn't seem capable of picking anything up off the floor. I guess I'll just have to learn to live with it. And so will you.

Anyway, that's a flavour of how a kid in the house is going to change your house, car, relationship and eating habits. If nothing else, there should be no surprises when the world as you knew it starts to fall apart. Now, let's get into some more detail, looking at the major milestones and challenges that a new dad will face, year by year.

2

THE BABY YEARS

The first couple of years with your first child are weird and wonderful. Weird, because it's impossible to imagine before-hand what it's like to be handed a small version of you and told, right, it's over to you. Wonderful, because babies are wonderful and then some. You could spend hours just staring at them, although you might be better off just grabbing some sleep. (The Golden Rule for new dads: never miss a chance for a kip.)

Anyway, here's what I think you'll find weird and wonderful during the first two years. Yes, I've written it tongue-in-cheek to give you a laugh. (You could do with one, every now and again.) But I'm not making any of this up. This is what it's like when a baby comes along. And it usually starts in the labour ward.

2.1 SURVIVING THE LABOUR WARD

This is a tricky place, full of landmines. You are literally get-ting an armchair ride in comparison to your partner. I've for-gotten half the things that happened since my kids were born; tiredness and an endless to-do list will do that to you. But I'll remember our hours in the maternity hospital for the rest of my life. It's one of the big, never-forgotten events, up there with the Leaving Cert and how you felt when someone told you where babies really come from. Here are my top tips.

Steer Clear of Telly

Some men watch *One Born Every Minute* to prepare themselves for the big day. This is like watching *The Blair Witch Project* in preparation for a camping trip. There is no point in terrifying yourself.

Others say the best way to prepare for the labour ward is to spend twenty-four hours with a constipated Rottweiler. I would change that to 'constipated Yorkshire Terrier', because there is every chance my wife will read this book. But you get the message.

It's No Joke

The delivery ward is no place for your stand-up comedy act. This is particularly important for Irish men, whose reaction to every situation is to act the clown. In fairness, a good sense of humour is a vital part of our toolbox, given that so many of us look like a bag of hammers. But the delivery ward is no joke. Your hilarious repertoire doesn't sound funny to a woman who is wondering if it's too late to have an epidural. The only thing that can make her laugh now is inhaled through a mask. So keep away from the gags.

This is especially true if the midwife is a bit of a looker and your partner reckons that the jokes are actually meant for her. Everything you say after that is going to get you in trouble. Here is a good rule of thumb – if the midwife looks remotely like Kate Hudson, don't even think of telling a joke.

It's increasingly likely, by the way, that the midwife will be a man. (Don't call him a midhusband.) You *will* feel weird, standing there while he peers at your partner's privates. You will feel an urge to relieve the tension by making some kind of blokeish quip. You should resist this urge.

Far better to watch a movie on your iPad. A few rom-coms might be in order, even if they make you want to die. I find *Marley & Me* is actually quite bearable, particularly when you are off your head on laughing gas. So remind her that sharing is caring. Alternatively, watch some porn. It's almost certainly the last sex you are going to see for a while.

No Tayto

Don't expect to eat well. This is an Irish hospital, the last place in the world you can expect to get healthy food. You'll be doing well to find a toasted panini.

Here are some food tips for your eighteen-hour ordeal. First, don't say that it's *your* eighteen-hour ordeal. If you don't know why, then I'm amazed you got a woman in the first place.

Secondly, steer clear of strongly flavoured crisps, because your partner's sense of smell during labour is set to Angry Wolf. (Don't use this comparison.) Finally, don't ask if it's okay if you pop out to McDonald's. It isn't. And it might be the one thing she will remember about the whole day. And you will never be forgiven.

The One Thing You'll Forget

New Dad leaves nothing to chance on the 'best route to maternity hospital' front. Seventy-six hours on Google Maps and two dummy runs later, you are ready for almost every eventuality, including a plague of locusts.

There's one detail you will overlook. This is captured in your partner's reaction when you arrive back from the underground car park after dropping her at the admissions desk in the hospital. 'What kept you, I'm having a baby, did you remember to get the suitcase out of the boot?' No, you forgot it. We all do. So, make sure to tape a piece of paper saying 'suitcase?' on the driver-side window in the run-up to the big day. Because that run back down to the car park can be a scary time.

Get Connected

Obviously the first thing you do on arrival at the delivery suite is check for decent Internet connection. You are a man and these things can't be helped.

Unfortunately, there is poor reception in a lot of delivery wards, which means you can't follow the minute-by-minute report of the Liverpool reserves playing Burnley. This child is wrecking your life already and it hasn't even been born. Try not to say this out loud. And put away the phone for a few hours.

Pokémon No

It doesn't matter if you are one of those couples who bonded over Pokémon Go. (Although it is a worrying sign that you mightn't be ready to have kids.) Telling your partner you are heading out for five minutes to play some geo-location game will only end one way – the loudest scream of the day in the delivery ward. At you, for trying to enjoy yourself when she is only three centimetres dilated. Sit back down there and ask if she'd like another glass of water.

Absolutely Useless

It's the age-old question. What can you do to make your-self useful, other than the glass of water mentioned above? A popular option is to offer your partner a massage. This is a good move as long as you have done it before. Otherwise you are making your massage debut on someone who would much rather you gave her a bottle of horse tranquillisers. You'll end up doing it all wrong.

If you can't be bothered to get some lessons in advance, just stick to rubbing her lower back and whispering, 'You're doing really well.'

A Record for All Time

Do you remember that urban myth during the video cassette years? Apparently someone video-taped their child's birth and played it on rewind to the child in later years, showing what might happen if he didn't behave.

Well, obviously I'm not suggesting you do that. Not when you can just record it on your mobile phone and show it on your Smart TV. (Get with the times, seriously.) Some people might say this is a cruel and barbaric practice. These people have never tried to discipline a child with a reward chart. You'll find details of reward charts further on in this book. Let's just say they're not the most effective way to control a toddler. So, don't forget to record the birth on your phone. You're going to need it. (Maybe ask for your partner's permission before tapping the red button though.)

You're Dead!

'It's a girl! Mother and daughter doing well.' The text you send from the corridor of the maternity ward will get some weird replies. Particularly if you send it to your ex by mistake, because you haven't slept for twenty-four hours. Yikes. Other women will be delighted, showering you with love and encouragement. Men? Not so much. Their messages will range from, 'You're dead now' and 'Call me in 5 years', to twenty-two versions of 'I'd hate to be you'. That's because a man finds it impossible to cope with a jubilant friend. There is nothing we can do about this.

2.2 WHAT'S IN A NAME?

I don't think it mattered what you called a child in the first half of the twentieth century. Both my mother and mother-in-law have completely different names to the ones that appear on their birth certs. Ask them why and they'll shrug and say that was just the way things were done. You gave your name a test-drive for twenty years; if you didn't like it you just picked another one. And who could blame you?

It's not like that any more. Not least because people tend to use their name in their email address and changing that is harder than time travel. So, whenever you set about choosing a name for your kid, you're doing it for keeps.

For what it's worth, our kids, Freda and Joe, are named after my wife's aunt and my uncle. This gives you a bit of choice; you're not stuck with just their grandparents' names.

Here are a few things to watch out for.

The Grandparents

It never hurts to name your kids after your parents. If nothing else, it's great emotional blackmail for a short spot of child-minding. (But she's named after you! And we'll be back in three weeks. A month, tops ...)

The question is, of course, which grandparent? That couple whispering furiously at each other in the bed next to you in the maternity hospital? They were both under the impression that the first boy would be named after *their* father. The only way to get around this is to pick a woman whose parents share a name with yours. Yes, that means there is a chance you are already related. But this is Ireland and these things happen on a small island.

Sorcha agus Óisín

Irish names have been in for a while. Particularly since they stopped being a signal that you are a mid-ranking official in the IRA. Here is the only thing you need to know about Irish names. People who didn't learn Irish in school for ten years have trouble pronouncing a word with three vowels in a row. So, if you name your kids Aoife, Eoin or Caoimhe, they'll never be able to get a job overseas. It will save you a fortune on flights to Australia. Look at you, all planning ahead.

Three Letters

A lot of people wonder why there has been a sudden rise in three-letter names like Ben and Ava. Until they decide to take their newborn on holidays. Those fifteen hours you spent writing a name like Nathaniel on your passport form/EHIC application/flight-booking/hotel-booking/travel insurance site? Well, that would have taken four hours if you'd called him Max. Reclaim your life with a three-letter child name. As for people who ask if it's okay to use Ben's full name and call him Benjamin? It isn't. Life is too short for long names.

Daniel and Emily

Here is a good reason to choose from the most popular boys' and girls' names in your country. The price of birthday cards.

Think about when your child goes to school. You will have to buy a birthday card for every kid in the class and if you give them cheapo ones from EuroGiant, people will mock your sprogs for being poor.

However, when your child shares a name with half the class, you can just recycle the ones she got at her party. Dear Emily, happy birthday, Emily, xx.

(You're so cheap.)

Telly Names

'Why did you call her Cersei?'

'She's my favourite character in *Game of Thrones*.'

'I haven't seen it.'

'Really? You're such a loser, I'm never going to talk to you again.'

Naming a child after a character from your favourite TV show is such a great way to put other people down. Who cares that you named your daughter after dangerous psycho Cersei Lannister? The important thing is you get a chance to show you are in touch with the zeitgeist. This TV name thing explains why the name Skylar cropped up in the last census. She was a leading character in *Breaking Bad*. What do you mean you've never seen it? You're such a loser. I'm never talking to you again.

Boy Named Sue

You're probably familiar with the story of the boy named Sue, in the Johnny Cash song of the same name. His dad called him Sue to toughen him up.

This won't work now, of course. The kids are all gender fluid these days and your son will probably end up as the coolest boy in the class. But giving your child a joke-ready name doesn't toughen them up in the long run. Take that from someone whose parents thought it would be a lark to call him Patrick Fitzpatrick. And yes, I've heard the joke about the two Irish gay men. 873 times.

Celebs

Here is an outline of why you shouldn't name a child after your favourite celebrity.

You name your child after your favourite celebrity. Four years pass. Said star goes on *Big Brother* to revive her career just as your daughter starts school. Said star has under-the-duvet sex with some former *Hollyoaks* star live on TV. Everyone is talking about it at school the next day because there is no way to stop kids watching what they want. The children notice that your daughter shares a name with the under-the-duvet-sex celeb.

Kids can be very cruel.

Zach and Ruth

You should consider a name from the Bible. A child called Zach or Ruth is such a good way of shouting, 'I'm rich, cool and middle-class.' And you don't even have to eat kale or buy an expensive composter. There is so much to like here.

There is actually a biblical name for kids born in Ireland. That name is Fintan. Seriously, it says here on the Internet that Fintan was the only Irish man who survived the great biblical flood. And we all know the Internet is never wrong about anything.

2.3 BRINGING BABY HOME

Well done – you managed to sit there and watch your partner push out your child. It's fair to say that was the easy bit, for you at least.

This is where things get a bit tricky.

I'll never forget the moments, coming out of the lift in the underground car park at the maternity hospital, as we set about bringing Freda home. I remember trying not to bang the car seat off the wall in case I'd hurt her. I was waiting for the nurse to come running down the stairs and say, 'There's been some mistake, people like you are clearly not ready to mind a child, hang on, I'll just get my coat and help you through the next four months.'

I remember thinking, *this is going to be tough*. Then another couple came out of the lift, trying to manage their newborn triplets between them. These things are all relative.

Here is what to expect when you bring baby home.

Visitors

Your house goes weirdly quiet when you first bring baby home. That's because all your relations say, 'We'll leave them alone now for a few days.'

As a result, twenty-seven members of your extended families arrive on day four. Yay! you shout through the tears. Naturally they 'don't want to be any trouble', so fourteen of them head out to the kitchen at the same time to make their own tea. Trying to help three aunties find the sugar after you have had no sleep is actually classified as cruel and unusual punishment by the UN. Don't worry, you'll see why.

A lot of visitors will want to sniff your baby's head and say, 'Ooh, I love the smell of a new baby.' Obviously, a well-adjusted person would love to see their little baby get that kind of attention. Unfortunately, you are a person who hasn't slept in four days. So there is every chance you will reply, 'How about I smear a mix of vomit and runny shite on her head, for an authentic new baby aroma?' Steer away from that. Word will go out that you're not coping with the new child at all. The result? Loads of people will call in unannounced to give you some help. They'll all want a sniff of her nibs. You can see where this is going. It just gets worse and worse.

Fantastic My Arse

Every second visitor will bring a baby toy that either plays a nursery rhyme or says 'You're fantastic!' in a deeply weird voice. (It's as if an American life coach moved into your house.) These toys sense when a tired person is walking past, trying not to make any noise in case they wake the baby. At this point the toy comes to life and says 'You're fantastic' in its outside voice. The feeling isn't mutual.

Worse again, there is no way to turn the shagging thing off. You have to wait for the battery to run out. By then, your child loves the toy as if it is a brother. So now you have to open the battery compartment with the smallest screwdriver in the world. And you still haven't had any sleep. The last thing you feel? Fantastic.

This Is War

You are a modern man who is fully committed to sharing the night-time duties with your partner. That's the public line and I recommend you stick to it. Privately, you'd try anything for a bit of extra kip. Don't feel bad about this. Your partner is at the same lark. This is war.

But don't worry, you have a key advantage. As a man, you come equipped with the conscience of a rattle-snake. That gives you the edge when it comes to lying there pretending to be asleep when the kid wakes at 3.30 a.m. Your partner will give it a go for a few minutes, but her female conscience will drag her down in the end.

Lips and Tips

Start practising biting your lip about two months before baby is born. That way you will be an expert in saying nothing when people start offering unsolicited baby tips.

One slip here and you could end up calling Auntie Clodagh a fat cow just because she said she knows a guy in Limerick who can get you some gripe water. You know the way she is.

She'll have all the cousins told that you're not coping at all. Worse again are the people with no kids who insist on sharing their theories on co-sleeping. You might want to practise biting your hand for that one.

You Live in a Dump

The biggest problem you face with a newborn in the house? Traffic management. People will be coming from far and wide to off-load boot-loads of baby junk that is clogging up their own place.

The one thing you won't get is the thing you need the most: a second garden shed to store eight high-chairs, 43,000 one-sies and seven Jumperoos that have a bit missing. You wouldn't get a quarter of that stuff if it was free to leave it at the dump. Don't worry. You'll be passing it on to some other eejit in no time.

Paternity Leave

Here's the worst thing about paternity leave. It exists. Before the baby arrives, you will see yourself as Bjorn, the Scandinavian hipster. You will enjoy telling everyone how you are looking forward to helping your partner through the difficult first two weeks.

Here's the thing, Bjorn the Scandinavian Hipster. Four days after baby comes home, you will text your boss, asking him to call over and publicly beg you to come back and save the company. That is because work is basically Club Med compared to looking after a newborn. But don't ever admit that to your beleaguered partner if she is the one left holding the baby.

Relaxation

Here's something to try close to the due date. Sit down on the couch. Get up some time later, when it suits you. You won't be doing that for a while. Not after the baby comes and your partner's sentences all start with, 'Could you get me the …'

This soon becomes 'Get me the …' and is further abbreviated to the name of the object within a month.

'Bib!'

'Spoon!'

If she is breastfeeding, it can feel like she is Father Jack out of *Father Ted*, sitting in the same spot for hours, barking out one-word sentences like arse and feck.

By the way, sometimes it can feel like your partner is just waiting for you to get comfortable before she sends you on your next mission. You could ask her if that is the case, if you fancy a fight.

2.4 NAPPY HAPPINESS

Nappies are another thing that will make you wonder how your parents managed, back in the day. Particularly when you are running to the bin with a nappy so toxic it's banned for use in war by the Chemical Weapons Convention. At least you are getting to throw it in the bin; your mother (let's face it, it was your mother) was washing and drying these things forty years ago, without a tumble dryer. So, the bottom line with nappies is they could be worse. Ask your mother if you don't believe me.

Nappy Dry Run

There are two key dry runs you need to make before baby arrives. The first is where you plot your route to the maternity hospital. (It's called a dry run because there is no risk of her waters breaking and making a mess of your new Hyundai.) The second, more important journey is the dry run to the nappy aisle in your nearest supermarket. That's not a trip you want to be making straight after the baby is born. (Everyone forgets to bring enough nappies to the hospital and that's where Dad is supposed to shine.)

Trying to find the right nappy for a thirty-minute-old baby is a tricky business. Trying to do it after eighteen hours in the delivery ward, where your partner called you a fuckity fuck because you told her it was too late to have an epidural, well that's never going to end well. Some of our best men have gone into that situation and still managed to come out with fourteen packs of pull-ups for a four-year-old. You'll be lucky to get away with just a fuckity fuck after that. So do a dry run with your partner and take a photo of the nappies you need to buy.

Which Nappy?

You'll probably need a small mortgage to put nappies on the first child. Why? Because your partner will want to swathe her baby in the limited-edition model, hand-woven in small batches in the Atlas Mountains by a team of artisan nappy makers. This is to get one up on her best friend, who only put her first child in Pampers. Don't worry, this extravagance won't last. After the two of you see what your darling child actually fires into a nappy, you'll realise there is no need for all the expense. If you're fortunate enough to have a second child, she'll be lucky to get wrapped up in old copies of *Hello!*

'But I made sure it was on properly!'

Says you, to your partner, as she cuts the latest shite-soaked onesie off your child. The truth is you didn't make sure it was on properly. There is a trick you need to do before you fasten the onesie back up, where you pull the elasticated pants bit of the nappy out around your child's thighs so that it makes a seal. You'd be surprised how much money this trick can save on replacement onesies, bathing products and divorce costs.

The Changing Bag

The main reason a woman wants to get pregnant is so she can spend a fortune on a designer changing bag. Okay, that's an over-statement, but not by as much as you'd think. What you need to decide is whether you are comfortable being seen in public with one of these. (They are basically a man-bag in brighter colours, with curves rather than straight lines.) If you are the type who doesn't care what people think, then you and the changing bag will get along just fine. Otherwise, I'd invest in a rucksack.

Random Nappy

You know that random nappy that's been lying around the back seat of your car for three months? Leave it there. The ironclad rule in this area is that no nappy ever goes unused. You'll see this rule in action when you drive Junior over to your mother's place on a Sunday morning, after a sleepless night, because the poor little guy had a bug.

Well, that bug has now moved to his arse. As a result, you've already gone through the three nappies you brought with you. Leaving the poor guy in his nappy will result in you facing a War Crimes Tribunal in The Hague. And then you remember – hang on, there's a nappy in the car. And then you remember again – hang on, I threw it out because I'm obsessed with cleanliness. Well, who's obsessed with cleanliness now? Your partner, as it turns out, when you bring her child home smelling like a septic tank. (It's always 'her child' when you are in the wrong.) So, here's that rule again. Never throw away the random nappy.

Changing Facilities

I'll never forget the first time I changed our daughter somewhere other than our house. She was about two months old. I was driving-test nervous.

It was a changing room in some shopping centre, small and windowless, the kind of place the cops would use as an interview spot if they were trying to force a confession. It smelled of all the children that had ever been changed in there before. And then I saw what looked like the changing table. It was a heavy slab of angry grey plastic, hinged onto the wall, folded in the vertical position. I pulled it down to the horizontal. This is going to snap back up against the wall, I thought, preparing for when I had to tell my wife that the changing table ate our child. Still, that would have been better than walking out there with an intact but unchanged daughter; wives hate that.

I strapped Freda down on the table (gently) and tried to rush it. Never rush a nappy change. It seemed like forever before I walked back out, nerves still jangling, with a freshly changed child.

What should have been simple, turned out to be an ordeal. Here's my advice. If, like me, you are inclined to be a bit anxious, take a trip into a changing room when you don't have a child in tow, just to get the lay of the land. Take note of what the table looks like, pull it down and convince yourself that it won't eat your child, get a feel for the little straps. Trust me, you don't want to try this for the first time with a stinking child under your arm.

The Holiday Nappy

You can always spot the couple on a first trip away with their baby. They're the ones who have checked in two bags full of nappies, as well as stuffing the buggy travel bag with more nappies to get one over on Michael O'Leary. (The buggy bag goes free and isn't weighed.)

But guess what? People in Spain and Portugal love their kids as well. So much so that they actually sell really good nappies, at reasonable prices, in supermarkets over there. So, if you are heading off for the first time, just pack enough in your hand luggage to get through the first day. (Lost luggage could make things very messy.) And don't worry, it's still okay to stuff the buggy bag with nappies, just to get one over on Michael O'Leary.

Time for Elimination Communication

Elimination communication is where you introduce your baby to the potty at about four months and discard the nappies. It is popular with some celebrities in the States, who have an army of people to go around cleaning up after their child.

The idea is that you learn to anticipate when your child is going to go and can rush them to the jacks. Here is the key thing you should know about elimination communication. You have a better chance of winning *Strictly Come Dancing* than you do of getting a crèche to accept a twelve-month-old without a nappy. Try this method, by all means. Just don't invite me to your house for a dinner party. I'll know why you chose a brown carpet. And it will put me right off my food.

2.5 TOO MUCH STUFF

Your tendency to buy stuff you don't need gets multiplied by forty-two once you have a child. This is because you head for a shopping centre on a rainy afternoon, just to get out of the house, and they're mad trying to sell you stuff in there. Worse again, you go to a giant home-store in a retail park and end up buying some 'I'll be broken in a week' garden decorations, just because there are loads of them.

There is no such thing as a free roof over your head on a rainy day. Every trip means buying stuff that makes your house that little bit smaller. (And your brain just a little bit crankier.)

That said, there are certain things you absolutely will need to help you through the early years. Here are my dos and don'ts, when it comes to stuff.

THE DON'T BUYS

Baby Monitors

Why do people spend a fortune on monitors? You already have a special device that will make a noise when your attention is required. It's called a baby. They come with ten pre-installed volume settings, from 'Did you hear a cry?' to 'I'm afraid to go in there.' If you reckon you live in a house so big that you can't hear your child crying, then hello, Kate Middleton and thanks for buying my book.

Baby monitors have only one use. Saving money on a babysitter when you leave Jack asleep in your hotel bedroom on a weekend break and sneak downstairs for a quick meal. Don't worry about the guilt. Everyone else in the dining room is at the same lark.

Buggy Mitts

It's freezing cold outside. Fantastic! You finally get to try out your €20 buggy mitts. You know the ones that stay fixed on the buggy, so you just slide your hands in and out without the hassle of taking off gloves. The next day it's 13 degrees outside (Ireland!). You put your hands into the mitts because there isn't room anywhere else on the buggy handle. You end up with very, very hot hands. You decide to take the buggy mitts off. It's not as easy as you think. The next day it's freezing again (Ireland!). You put the mitts back on the buggy again. It isn't as easy as you might think. It's certainly not as easy as putting on your gloves. You throw the buggy mitts in the bin.

Weaning Spoon

Here is one thing we know for certain. The human race has survived and evolved into the most successful species on earth without the help of weaning spoons that cost a tenner. And yet, people buy weaning spoons for a tenner. (You'll need three, because when you have kids, everything is lost all the time.) Actually, all you really need is some patience, a bib for the child, a washable body suit for yourself and a roll of plastic sheeting to put under the kitchen table. That should come to €2. The €28 saved will keep you in decent wine for a week. You'll need that at weaning time. Unless you rate 'prising scrunched-up broccoli out of the floorboards' as one of life's great pleasures.

Russian Doll Baby Bag

You know, the one that's a big bag with a number of 'handy' smaller bags inside it. Because if there's one thing a first-time dad has, it's enough time to pack two different bags when he is heading out for the day. 'It's so handy, I can just take this slightly smaller bag out in the restaurant,' said no one who ever tried to pack a bag while changing a nappy on a six-month-old wriggle-meister and talking to work on the phone. This only ever ends one way. An ad on DoneDeal saying: 'For Sale: Two Smallish Bags, used once, couldn't stop cursing.'

Teething Necklace

I'm not sure if an amber teething necklace eases the pain when little Amy is getting her first set of gnashers. I *am* sure you have to survive on four minutes of broken sleep when a child is teething and you won't be able to deal with all the necklace-related comments. So, if you do decide to go with the necklace, you should hand out the following printed message to every-one you meet. *Thank you for your interest in my child. Yes, I am aware of the tiny choking risk associated with the necklace. And no, it doesn't mean we've 'gone all hippy', all of a sudden.*

The Extra Slings

Every parent has good things to say about the sling they use to carry their child. It's the other slings, the ones they don't use that cause the problem. Particularly when there are eight of them lying around your small house. Research shows this isn't caused by men, because we're not that bothered about how we look. That's why you'll often see one of us out and about with little Sophie strapped into a sling that doesn't go with our shirt. (Mom wouldn't even think of it.)

Some might think this is a fashion no-no. We reckon we're getting plenty of Yummy Mummy saucy glances for being hands-on sling Dad. So don't feel sorry for us.

Baby Wipe Warmer

Seriously, it's a thing. You can buy one for around €40. They are popular with a lot of people in the States. But then so is Donald Trump. I don't remember being a baby myself, but when it comes to temperature and bum-wipes, I'd be one of those people who likes it as cold as possible. So do you, particularly when it's less than two days since your last chicken jalfrezi. Bear that in mind when thinking about the state of your child's bum. And put her wipes in the fridge.

THE DO BUYS

A Decent Washing Machine

One thing is clear after child number two comes on board. Your house is essentially a few rooms attached to a medium-sized launderette. Not just that. Research shows that 73% of parents split up because there is no clean onesie for little Jack.* So spend money on a decent washing machine with plenty of capacity. And insist on an industrial standard tumble-dryer while you're at it. This isn't just about clean clothes; it's also about domestic peace. And you can't put a price on that.

* I made this up. But it's still true.

A Thermometer

You see, there's your first mistake already. Any guy who thinks he can get by with only one thermometer is on a fast track to failure.

You need at least three thermometers. The first one costs €9.99. This seems fine. And then your cousin says she thought she read a thing on Facebook saying that model gave a faulty reading for a child in Holland, who went on to suffer from a cold for three days. You can't sleep for a week with the worry. So you buy one for about €40, as recommended by your GP. This seems fine until your aunt says that people who study medicine are mad for the booze. So you remortgage the house and buy a thermometer designed by two scientists head-hunted from the CERN particle accelerator project in Switzerland. It never gives the same reading twice. You end up using the thermometer you bought for €9.99. So now you know.

The Whiteboard

You're nothing these days without a mini whiteboard in the kitchen. This is not so you can organise your crazy life. There isn't any need, given that Google Calendar is on every device you own. (It will be available on your expensive washing machine one of these days.)

The real purpose of the whiteboard is to show visitors that you are the best parents in the world. Who cares that Ruby isn't really going to ballet three times a week? Or that Conor doesn't actually have a season ticket for Old Trafford. The important thing is that other parents come into your house and think they are doing a bad job themselves. Well done you!

The Sand

Jean Paul Sartre famously said that hell is other people. That's because he never visited Portmarnock. Because then he would have said that hell is other people on an Irish beach. It all feels very Costa Del Sophisticated until the guy next to you buries his kid's nappies in the sand. You take a photo and send it in to Joe Duffy, but this doesn't make you feel any better.

The trick is to steer clear of the beach where possible and instead build one out the back of your house. A paddling pool and sand table should do the trick for kids under five. And you can knock back cheap rosé without worrying about the drive home. There is so much to like here.

The Second Shed

You're not seriously planning to go through all of this with one shed? Rookie error. The reason is simple. If a child doesn't own seven scooters by the age of four, you are officially the worst parent of all time. (This has been contrived by the scooter industry; there is nothing you can do to stop it.)

Worse still, your memory goes blank every time you walk into Aldi. That's why you also own three sets of garden furniture and two unopened gazebos. Buy a second shed. If nothing else, it doubles the number of places you can go to escape the madness. Excellent.

The Roof Box

There is only one problem with a roof box on your car. You can't have two of them. (We're the species that put a man on the moon. Someone should look into that.) Some say a roof box causes an annoying, whistling sound in the car. I say that blocks out the sound of the kids. (No kids, we're not there yet.)

A decent roof box costs about €300. A decent relationship counsellor costs ten times that. Bear that in mind. Because 56% of relationships fail soon after a man tells his partner there isn't room for a third case of onesies on their weekend trip to Galway.*

So buy the box and enjoy the whistling sound.

* I made this up too. But it's still true.

The Back Aid

Here's something to remember if you get roped into a litter

sweep as part of a Tidy Towns campaign. Don't hand back your picker-upper. You know, the long stick with a claw at the end for picking up rubbish. That can determine your quality of life for the next ten years. Carry one around the house and you can clean up after your kids. Try to live without one and you'll end up putting your osteopath's kids through college.

Here's the thing about kids. They always have something in their hand, which they drop when you cajole them to clean up a previous mess. It never ends.

Plastic

No, not the credit card. Although you will need that more than ever. Plastic here means plastic bags. Don't leave home without at least four in your pocket. And we're not talking nappy sacks here. They have a try-too-hard scent that is weirdly worse than baby shite.

Bin liners are more like it. Just perfect in our local shopping centre, when little Joe gives his onesie the old vomit-poo one-two. You can't throw it in the bin, because that's just the kind of episode that will end up on YouTube, headlined 'Deadbeat Dad ruins everything'. Walk around with it in your hand and someone will contact security. There is a lovely first memory for little Joe. 'I wasn't shoplifting', you'll be telling him to no avail, in ten years' time.

No, what you need to do is double wrap the foul onesie in two of your plastic bags and head for home. That way, you still have two bags to double-wrap the replacement onesie, when little Joe repeats the trick five minutes later. That's usually how the old vomit-poo one-two pans out. You have been warned.

Wet Wipes

What is the great achievement of the human race? Putting a man on the moon? Fig rolls? Not even close. It's wet wipes. You must never, ever run out of them. It can take a while before you really appreciate the beauty of these damp slices of paper. Particularly in the first few weeks of a child's life, when you are spending more on wet wipes than you are on wine. (How did that happen?)

But then at four o'clock one morning, just after your child has turned himself into a juvenile shite bomb, you ask the Big Question: How did people get by before wet wipes? The Big Answer? Not very well. Ever wonder why those people in old black and white photos look so miserable? No wet wipes. Well, that and the ever-present threat of disease and violent death. But mainly the lack of wet wipes.

Spare Sippy Cups

There is a black hole in the universe where sippy-cup tops disappear. I'm not suggesting this black hole was invented by the sippy-cup industry to make us buy new ones. But that's only because Big Sippy-Cup has great lawyers and I'd hate to see them angry.

Eventually you end up with four cups and no lids. At this point you might say, 'She's old enough now, I'll give her some milk in an open cup.' Five minutes later you are on the way out to buy a new cup. Not to mention a new carpet. Spare yourself the journey and get your hands on some spare sippy cups the first time. (Thirty-five should do.)

The Parenting Books

The bad news is there are millions of books out there promising to help you rear your child. The good news is that one of them is bound to back up your crackpot notions about parenting. (It might even be this one!) So keep reading until you find that book and then tell everyone, 'Look, I was right all along!'

A Rubbish Skip

I'm writing this on a Monday morning, with a skip full of stuff ready for collection in the front garden. The attic, where I do my writing, is pretty empty; it's just me and the cat now. The whole loading the skip thing took about five hours; the clutter reduction has added five years to my life. Two simple rules when you hire a skip:

1: Choose the size you want and then book the next size up. You have more stuff than you think. (That breadmaker from Aldi, what were you thinking?)

2: If you find something you forgot you had, put it in the skip. (Unless it contains codeine. Never throw out anything with codeine when there are kids in your life.)

2.6 ANY CHANCE OF SOME SEX?

It was probably sex that got you into this situation in the first place. I hope it was memorable, because you might have to survive on that memory for a while. The problem isn't that your partner won't be up for it when there is a small baby in the house. (Even though she probably won't.) The issue is that *you* mightn't feel like it, what with having no sleep and fighting off the endless colds and bugs that seem to follow a baby around.

Not feeling like it can be a problem for blokes, because 'feeling like it' was always one of your things. When that goes, you can start to feel a bit old and bitter. It's the kind of thing that could get you down if you thought it was permanent.

It isn't. The same phrase that applies to most of the hard times in baby-land – it will pass – applies to the dip in your sex-life.

I won't tell anyone to be patient here. That isn't really how sex works. But hopefully you'll get a laugh and a couple of insights on what I observed about sex after baby arrives, followed by a look at the things you can do to rekindle the romance. (My wife has asked me to add that none of this has anything to do with our sex life, but is based on things my friends told me after a couple of drinks. I can neither confirm nor deny this.)

So let's start by talking about sex.

Induce Me, Baby

Don't believe everything you read. A new baby around the house doesn't really affect your sex life. It's not like you were swinging from the rafters during the final months of pregnancy. Unless one of you works as a trapeze artist, because there was definitely no sex. Except of course for induce-me sex. That's the one where he pretends to find her attractive and she pretends to believe him, because she will do anything to get this shagging baby out!! Twelve hours later and still no baby. They decide to do it again. Twice in one day. That's going to seem like some kind of orgy after the baby arrives. (Try twice in one year.)

I'll Be Your Substitute

It's not easy being a new parent. No more boozy nights or weekend breaks or anything that you might describe as a bit of fun. So it's no surprise that a lot of couples resort to the one thing they can still enjoy together – chocolate. A nice Crunchie is just the thing when the kids have been packed off to bed. Chocolate certainly beats sex, because you can enjoy it while watching Netflix, which is about all you're good for.

A word of warning for the lads. Don't try to match your partner's chocolate intake if she is breastfeeding. She is in the business of producing sweet milk for the little one; you'll just end up with man-boobs and fat knees. That's not a great look if you are planning to ever have sex again.

Hurry On!

A baby in the cot can spice things up. Mainly because it means the end of having sex in the bedroom. Unless you are turned on by your partner hissing, 'Enough moaning – you wake him, you own him.'

The result is very often a quickie in the sitting room. (Top tip – never buy a second-hand couch from a couple with a small baby.) This isn't just a quickie because babies seem to sense sex and wake up just as you are getting to the good bit. It's also because relations have a habit of dropping in unannounced, letting themselves in so they don't wake baby.

Hence the rush. There are some moments you would like to share with your mother-in-law. This isn't one of them.

This Means Divorce

You need to choose your words carefully when it comes to post-baby action. Here is a typical exchange after your partner gives birth. Him: 'Let's do it.' Her: 'But you couldn't possibly find me attractive.'

Tricky. You'd want to have a response figured out in advance, because anything you say off the top of your head will probably end up getting repeated in the divorce court. Particularly if it's 'You know, they say that sex is a great way to lose weight.' That's curtains.

Sex Toys

Looking for a sex toy to improve your love life after baby arrives? I recommend a screwdriver and some WD-40.

It's not what you think. (I'm not even sure what you think.) You see, the old seduction tricks like whisking her off to Paris or pretending to like romcoms are out the window. Sorry about the brutal truth, but nothing turns Mom on faster than a guy who can assemble a Jumperoo in three minutes flat. Fix the bedroom door squeak that's been waking Junior and she'll be all over you like a cheap suit. Again, my apologies if this seems a bit harsh. But at least it beats pretending to be delighted that *Pretty Woman* is on BBC One at nine o'clock.

If you'd like some tips, I've included everything I know about DIY towards the end of the book. Don't worry, it's a short section.

Foreplay? Hilarious.

There was a time when you had time to get in the mood. (Usually the time it took to drink a bottle of wine says you, ruefully.) Now it's probably the time it takes to say, 'Okay, he's snoring, get 'em off you.' The Puritans had more foreplay than that.

Of course you can follow those nicey-nicey sex guides, which suggest you slowly seduce your partner with gentle touches and caresses throughout the day. Later that night, the curtains are closed, the kids are asleep and you both have only one thing on your minds – finding the right way to say, 'I'm a new kind of knackered, can we do this some other night?' Damn you, nicey-nicey sex guides for getting our hopes up.

Seriously, foreplay is for people with too much time on their hands. Every second you are working your busy hands over each other is another second that your youngest could wake up in the cot and decide the last thing he needs is a baby sister.

I've heard that some couples wear earplugs during sex, so they can ignore the crying. Here's how that plays out:

'You make me so horny.'

'Did you just call me Lorna?'

'Yes. Yes.'

'Who's Lorna?!!'

You might want to avoid earplugs.

Contraception

Yes, I know, your partner has just given birth to the best form of contraception known to humankind. How could you possibly make another one, with this one crying her head off for eighty-three hours a night?

Well, ask any midwife. Apparently the most common phrase in the delivery ward is, 'Would it have killed you to put on a fucking condom?' (Followed by 'And no, I don't want another fucking back rub.')

A condom is far and away the best form of contraception in these circumstances. Here is a three-step guide to how it works. 1. You try to put on the condom without waking the child in the cot next to you. 2. You fail. 3. There goes any chance of sex for another night.

Pick a Night

A friend of mine used to call it Batman Suit Night. (It definitely takes all kinds.) It's where you take the seduction out of sex and pick a night that it's going to happen, no matter how tired you are.

The problem here is what night to pick. All I can say is that Tuesday and Wednesday nights are out because of the Champions League. I hear a lot of women find it a turn-off when their partner says, 'Hang on a sec, I just want to see if Dunphy thought that was a penalty.' Apparently, a lot of women are not turned on by a mention of Eamon Dunphy.

Extra Hot

Baby in the house? I'd steer clear of any sort of dirty talk. Asking your partner if she fantasises about trying something new in bed will lead to a one-word answer – sleep.

She has probably had eighteen minutes' kip in the past

month. If my memory of newborns is correct, she has a small amount of eight-day old vomit in her ear. It isn't hers. Suddenly you creep up behind her in the kitchen and whisper, 'You've been a very naughty girl' in her ear. That's never going to end well.

You'd be better off joining the priesthood. With that approach, you're going to be celibate anyway, so you might as well get the free meals and handy trips to Rome.

Now is not the time to spice up your love life. The chances are that one or both of you will fall asleep before fireworks time. So don't be wasting time with saucy sentences.

Something for the Weekend

You will be subjected to Sexy Weekend Break ads. These show a bath-robed couple in some 4-star hotel, as an overly cheerful bell-boy delivers croissants and coffee. It's pretty clear they've been at it all night.

Not that you care. All you see are the crisp, white sheets. It doesn't look as if there is any baby puke on them. Wow. You ditch the kids for the first time and head off for some crisp white sheets. It's all going to plan until you both fall asleep at the table in the restaurant on the first night. Sexy! Still, there's no need to be embarrassed. The restaurant is full of couples with kids who fell for the crisp white sheets. And they're all asleep too.

Well, that's the end of the sex counselling for this book. I hope that has solved all your sex problems. Joking aside, it varies from person to person, and you will probably have to feel your way through it. (Sorry.)

2.7 KEEP THE ROMANCE ALIVE

Of course, it takes more than good sex to keep your relationship on course. (At least that's what men say in public.) If I had one piece of advice to give to new dads, it would be to remember two things – your partner is probably as tired as you are and she probably still loves you.

It might be a good idea to get that tattooed on your eyelids, as a reminder before you start your day. Because the stress and anxiety of keeping the show on the road with a new baby around will change your relationship.

I remember a friend of mine telling me this before our first baby arrived. I had no concept of what she was talking about until we found ourselves in the same situation. The one thing I've learned is it requires a conscious effort to keep the peace.

Here's a look at some dos and don'ts in the relationship arena.

Cyber Flirting

A lot of people recommend flirty texts and saucy photos to keep the magic alive. They've obviously never tried it. Otherwise they'd realise the dangers of Autocorrect Bingo. That's what happens when you are trying to send an affectionate message to your partner while juggling a three-month-old in your arms.

My guess is the person who designed the autocorrect feature on your phone had just been dumped by his girlfriend and he decided to take it out on the world. So good luck explaining a text saying, 'Incense? You're such a hippo.'

As for photos, well here's the problem with sending a saucy

selfie. Science shows that a one-year-old child can find any item on your phone by accident with just three clicks and a swipe. Good luck with that explanation. 'Mom was really, really warm that day. And she's always wanted to be a nurse.'

It's Chore Day Off?

Some suggest you should give the washing machine a day off and focus on each other. What's wrong with that? Well, you tried it once and it nearly ended in divorce. Research shows that if you leave the laundry basket alone for a day it will actually start talking to you.

'I'm very full', 'I'm getting a bit stinkier', 'You realise you'll have to do fifteen loads tomorrow just to make up for this, don't you?'

There really is no getting away from laundry. One solution is to do a double-shift of chores today, so you can free up time tomorrow. So, you stay up until 11 p.m. doing another four washes. The only thing you are good for the following day is to appear as an extra in *Night of the Wrecked Zombies III*. Is that the laundry basket saying, 'I could have told you that was going to happen'? Probably. The laundry basket, it rules your relationship now.

Presents

Buying cheap lingerie for your partner is a bad idea at any time of the year. There's a chance they'll look tatty on herself and you'll try to help by saying, 'That's weird, they looked amazing on your one in the poster, in the shop.'

You need to look beyond the marketing. Lidl once referred

to their Valentine's lingerie collection as 'The Look of Love'. Buy some for your partner and you could end up calling it 'Four Nights on the Couch (By Myself)'.

Here is a quick note for any women reading this, on the lookout for a quick and easy gift. We have nothing against wallets. A man can't have too many as far as we're concerned. And if it comes down to a choice between that and socks, it's wallets every time. I suppose what we're getting at is this. Is there any chance we could have a home-brew kit? We've always wanted to make our own beer.

A Weekend Away

Is there anything better than a weekend away from the kids? (A fortnight says you, packing your bag.)

Seriously, there is a lot to be said for a quickie break. (Hopefully there will be time for more than a quickie, says you again, already out in the car, ready to go.) The rules are simple. Choose a location far enough away that your partner won't be tempted to go home when you get a WhatsApp from the babysitter saying the baby was a bit sad after you left. (Wouldn't it be worse if the baby didn't miss you?)

The next rule is don't get on a plane – you'll only get stressed at the airport and start on the wrong footing. I like a one- or two-hour drive to the destination, it gives us time to relax and catch up with each other.

And finally, don't get upset that you fell asleep after two pints and woke up in your clothes the next morning. It happens to all of us.

Hugging

Tricky. A lot of experts recommend a hug to keep the intimacy on track. Mind you these are Internet experts, so you might as well be taking a blue pill that came in a jiffy bag from a company called FoamingAtTheMouth.com.

There is a problem with hugs. Let's just say that a hug can mean different things to different people. Particularly if one is a man and the other is a woman. I'm not sure what a woman is thinking when she goes in for a hug. But here's what most men think: 'She is either doing this because she read on a website that it's good for our relationship, or else we're going to have sex. I'll be really disappointed if it's the first one.'

A Love Letter

You could do worse than trade love letters. It is the only form of contact left to parents which cannot be used to pass on messages about the children. Face it, an affectionate text or Viber message goes something like this: 'I don't say this often enough, but you really are my soulmate. P.S. Jack's poo is very hard, did you defrost the stewed pears from the freezer? P.P.S. If the answer to the last question is no, please defrost some pear from the freezer in time for his tea. P.P.P.S. Seriously, don't forget. P.P.P.P.S You're my hippo. xx'

The problem here is we are out of letter-writing practice. The only time we write one these days is to beg some school principal to bump our Ava up the list. Not to worry, the Internet has you covered. There are loads of stock letters out there which will do the job nicely. Most of them are written by Americans, so make sure to substitute in the word 'grand' everywhere you see 'awesome'.

Will We Have Another One?

From talking to friends, it's clear that men decide they are done having kids one child before their partner has had enough. I think this is an evolutionary thing and there isn't much you can do about it. Basically, most women are programmed to crave small cute things, even if those small cute things don't sleep for eighteen months and tend to throw up in restaurants.

Again, from talking to friends, I reckon most men think it's game over once they have a second kid. As a result you should plan for a bit of conflict when your second child reaches their first birthday. The conflict often goes like this:

Your partner: 'Come on, we'll have another one.'

You: 'No.'

Your partner: 'But they're so cute and cuddly.'

You: 'We haven't slept in three years.'

Your partner: 'I'm not kidding here, I'm going to find someone else to have a child with. What's your answer to that?'

You: 'A vasectomy. And ask your new boyfriend if he wouldn't mind picking up the other two from the crèche.'

So, if you want to keep things sweet in your relationship, I'd start planning a better approach than the one above. Because you don't really want another man raising your two kids. (Or do you?)

2.8 FENCE MENDING

It's funny how you can lose the habit of doing something nice for each other when there's a bit of a niggle in the air. But, at the risk of sounding like a Californian who has been at the happy pills, it's nice to be nice. Doing a good deed for your partner isn't just about brownie points that can be cashed in when you want to go on that weekend to Berlin.

A good deed, just for the sake of it, lifts the mood in the room. It mightn't be reciprocated there and then, particularly if you are engaged in a bit of fence mending, but these things have a habit of coming back around. And if that coming around leads you to a departure lounge heading to Berlin, great. But everyone's a winner when you make an effort.

Here are a few dos and don'ts to get you thinking on the subject. Feel free to say you thought of them yourself.

The Telly

Never, ever go for brownie points by allowing your partner access to the remote control. Why? Because women are capable of watching TV and looking at their phones at the same time. (Or so it seems.) So, while she sniggers at some video on Facebook, you'll end up stuck watching *Hollyoaks*. There is nothing you can do about this, because you can't complain when trying to mend fences. *Hollyoaks* is popular with a lot of people, but none of them are over sixteen or have an Adam's apple. It could put you off fence mending for good.

The Task

Women love the old saying 'For every job a man does, he creates another two.' Possibly because it's true. There are two ways you can react to this. One is to announce you are no longer going to do any jobs around the house because your partner is busy enough without giving her more to do. This is a good way to create extra work. For a divorce lawyer.

The other reaction is to actually do a job that does not create another job. The good news is there must be a way to do this. The bad news is I'm a man so I haven't a clue what it is.

The Gift

A present should cost between €30 and €100. Any less and you're a cheapskate. Any more and you're just throwing money at the problem rather than using your imagination. (Don't ask why this is true, I just write what I see.)

Forget about buying cosmetics. Unless you think you have a good answer for, 'Are you suggesting I look old?'

Buying lingerie or sex toys is a complete no-no. Unless you fancy bumping into your spinster aunt in town with a Rampant Rabbit in your hand. (We've all been there.)

Suffer Baby, Suffer

Here is the golden rule of sending your partner on a spa break – you must endure hardship while she is away. (Saying you will suffer from acute loneliness is corny and will only get you in trouble.)

So, don't bring the kids to see your mother, because that could be seen as you taking a break. If you drink half a bottle of wine when the kids go to bed, make sure to drink the other half and ditch the bottle before she comes home. (We know you're up to it.)

Finally, don't mention that the three-year-old woke in the middle of the night because there was a shark in the wardrobe. That could be seen as moaning. That's minus fifty brownie points right there. So it isn't enough that you have to suffer. You have to suffer in silence.

Compliments

You don't want to get carried away on the compliments front. Making more than two positive comments a day about her appearance is usually greeted by the worst news a man can ever hear: 'Thanks, but I'm still not having sex with you tonight.' Gutted.

And then there is the 'I love you', 'I love you too' exchange familiar to all parents. This is where you tell her she is the best mom in the world and she says you are the best dad in the world. This works nicely. Until one day your 'best mom in the world' line is greeted with silence. Nothing. You've just lost your title as best dad in the world. Anything you say to try to reclaim it will only sound needy. And needy is never sexy. So don't go there.

Romantic Meal

It's your night to cook dinner. You go for broke with Beef Wellington served with a red wine reduction. She's going to love this, says you, as she walks in the door and asks, 'What are the kids going to eat?'

Tricky. She makes a good point. You've been so diligent in rearing the kids that they don't like McDonald's. What a nightmare. She might sit there and enjoy her Beef Wellington while the kids sulk through Weetabix. And you might get a WhatsApp message from Jennifer Lawrence saying, 'My place, 9 p.m., don't be late sexypants.' That's how likely it is. So here's the rule for brownie-point meals. Make them mashable. (Kids love mashable and it's made for spoon-feeding.)

The Lie-In

The first rule of 'Giving Her a Lie In'? You have to go all the way. Don't be getting excited now – this has nothing to do with sex.

Going all the way here means getting the kids out of the house. Otherwise one of the little tykes will escape into the bedroom and sit on her head. You're well into negative brownie points territory there. The second rule of 'Lie In' is known as 'the Hug Drop'. This is where you call in back home at 10 a.m., so that your partner can have a ten-minute cuddle with them before drifting back to sleep. You take them out again until lunchtime. That is actually worth fifty squillion brownie points.

2.9 MONEY PROBLEMS

The average cost of rearing a child in 2017, from birth to the age of twenty-four, was €105,000. That's enough to give a man erectile dysfunction.

It can sometimes feel as if you are spending most of this in the early years. Particularly if you are a double-earning couple who sit down and do the sums on childcare before the kid arrives. Basically, you'll need to earn €30,000 (gross) to pay for two kids in full-time childcare in Ireland (at the time of writing). You could easily go from the free and easy days of never checking your current account balance, to dipping into your overdraft every month. It's another strain on a relationship that is already bent out of shape by a lack of sleep and 375 decisions a day.

Here is a sideways glance at where the money goes during the early years. It might even save you a few quid!

Wet Wipes

Research shows that Irish parents spend 75% of their income on wet wipes every year.* Why? Guilt – anything less than 110% pure water ones, hand-crafted by wet wipe experts in Switzerland, is the height of bad parenting. Those 98% water ones with a tiny bit of perfume? You might as well be dumping your baby on the steps of an orphanage.

The trick is to use fewer wet wipes. This means the return of 'The Cloth'. You know, the stinky damp thing your mother had hanging off the tap. Use that instead of a wet wipe to clean small faces and hands. That's a ten-grand saving right there.

* Made up. My guess is it's actually higher.

Buggy

The buggy has two main uses. 1: Ferrying your kids around. 2: Making other parents feel inadequate because they can't afford a Bugaboo Cameleon. (It's so much cheaper than buying a new BMW.) If you can't afford one of those, buying a second-hand buggy is still a great way to rub your friend's face in it. (You feel so sorry for his little Jack, being pushed around in a Greco.)

Second-hand buggies might not always stay in vogue. Not if you live in Ireland, the only country in the world which puts the year on car registration plates. That's how snobby we are. It's only a matter of time before we have buggy licence plates showing when it was first purchased. And who wants to be seen pushing around a 2012 UPPAbaby? Talk about mortification.

Childcare

Good news. The government has promised to reduce the burden of childcare over the next few budgets. Bad news. They are the government. If you really believe cheap childcare is anything more than an election ruse, please send us your credit card details, as our uncle the former president of Bugandanzia would like to deposit $100 million in your account so it can be used to hug polar bears.

Look, there is still only one way to cut childcare costs. Pay a gorgeous young Spanish woman 140 euro a week to rear your kids. This is proving very popular with Irish dads. Irish moms? Not so much.

Nappies

I read recently that it costs almost €600 for disposable nappies in the first year of your child's life. There are a few ways people try to reduce this.

For example, anyone with small boys might notice that a wet nappy is still perfectly dry at the back. So why not turn it around and use it again? Because someone will find out and you'll be the subject of a TV3 documentary called *Super Scrimping Parents from Hell.* So that's out.

Here is another false economy. You buy 300 size-four nappies in the supermarket because they are on special offer. Your sneaky baby has a growth spurt on the way home in the car. You put him in the size four nappies anyway. They can't hold all the wee. You decide to have another baby to use up the size fours. That will only cost you a fortune in the long run.

Doctor's Fees

Yes, your child now has free GP visits up to the age of six, which is why some parents sold their house and moved into their local doctor's waiting room. At least that is how it seems.

I'm not suggesting you try this. Neither am I suggesting you should use your child's GP medical card to get a free consultation for yourself. That would be unethical and maybe even illegal. But I know that certain people bring their perfectly healthy child to the doctor and end the visit with, 'Now that I'm here, you'd never have a quick look at my knee.' Just saying.

Clothes

You might be familiar with the term 'Gentleman's Family'. That's when you have two kids, a boy and a girl. It's a good thing, apparently. Unless you are the second kid, and a boy. There you are in the family photo, aged two and a half, dressed in your sister's tights. They're not even navy. Some parents just can't resist squeezing another few months out of the eldest one's clothes.

Here's the lowdown on dressing your little boy in his sister's clothes:

1: Vests and onesies are good up to one.

2: Coats and hats work up to two.

3: There is a chance he'll blame you for anything that happens to him for the rest of his life if you put him in the dress from *Frozen*. Particularly if you put a photo of this up on Facebook for a laugh. Even if it is very funny.

Plastic Property

I'm not suggesting that toy houses are expensive. But it is still possible to find a three-bed semi-D in Ireland that is cheaper than a Little Tikes Playhouse. (They're the plastic things that crop up in people's back gardens once their first kid hits one.)

The problem is, once your little tykes get used to the plastic house, they'll want to trade up to a plastic castle.

The best thing is to scare them off property with a spooky house story. It was a stormy day in 2007. Mom and Dad signed the mortgage forms for their lovely new house. And now they are imprisoned there forever by evil bankers. It would be funny if it wasn't true.

The Voucher Pyramid

You should tell your partner about the Smyth's Voucher arrangement. This is where a group of moms get together and agree that everyone will give everyone else a €20 voucher for their child's birthday present. (If you think dads have anything to do with organising presents for their kids, then think again.) So, with ten kids in the circle, you get 9 x €20 vouchers for your little Sophie's birthday. You give her three of them and keep six to give to other kids in the circle, when their birthday comes around. Good, isn't it?

Well, yes, as long as Sophie is one of the older kids in the circle. Otherwise, it's a pyramid scheme, where you get stuck with a load of vouchers you can't pawn off on the older kids, because they will be out of date by the time the next birthday rolls around. You can't give them all to Sophie, or she'll think you're loaded. That's a shortcut to bankruptcy right there.

Here's a trick if you have one of the youngest kids in a Smyth's Voucher Circle and are stuck with some useless bits of paper. Hang around the door of the classroom below your Sophie's at school and see if you can flog them at face value to someone in a voucher circle down there. The golden rule here is to find a bigger eejit than yourself.

Beautiful Baby?

It isn't unusual to look at your child and wonder if you can make a few quid off her. Particularly if she's cute. I wouldn't bother with Beautiful Baby competitions, you'll probably end up on a TV exposé called *Awful Dads stuck in the 1980s*, and everyone will hate you.

There is of course one Beautiful Baby competition it's still okay to enter. It's called Facebook. You post a pic of your newborn up there and everyone says how cute she looks, even though all babies look a bit like squirrels until they hit the three-month mark.

Everyone who likes the photo will then use it as an excuse to post old photos of their own kid, complete with a passive-aggressive comment along the lines of 'but I still think mine is cuter #onlymessing #seriously.' (Actually, that's just aggressive-aggressive.) There is a lot of money to be made from this competition. As long as your name is Mark Zuckerberg.

2.10 THAT'S WEIRD!

I was the last of my circle of friends to have kids. One by one, not long after I got their 'baby born' text from the labour ward, I'd watch them slowly fade away into this other world I didn't understand. It struck me that some of the things they said and did were downright weird. Now I have kids myself, so I understand.

Here are some of the weird things you will start doing.

The Butt Sniff

We've all been there. One minute you are having a nice conversation with your lifelong friend. The next minute she picks up her new baby and sniffs his butt. There's only one solution to that. A new friend. Seriously, butt-sniffing is a deal-breaker in human beings. You're not even comfortable with it when it comes to dogs.

This all changes when you have a baby. There he is sitting on the ground with that goofy grin. He could be just happy. Or maybe he had a poo. You could pick him up, peel back two layers plus the nappy in an attempt to see the poo. But who has the time for that with a six-month-old in your life? Welcome to the butt-sniffers. And don't forget to ring your old friend to tell her you want her back.

Beautiful Tears

Reckon no one ever feels happy at the sound of a crying child? Think again. Or maybe just have a child. Because sometimes the sound of a roaring child is the most beautiful sound of them all. As long as the child isn't yours.

This is particularly the case on holidays. You're lying awake in the middle of the night, enjoying the peace, thinking this couldn't get any better. Then a baby starts crying in the apartment next to yours. You imagine the parents dragging their sorry arses out of bed to deal with it. You feel weirdly elated because it isn't you. There is a name for this feeling. Psychopath. So keep that weird elation to yourself.

Crying on a Friday

Offices can be weird places on a Friday afternoon. Half the place is buzzing in anticipation. The other half sits there crying their eyes out. They're the ones with young kids. Another glorious work week is coming to an end and it's back to the grind of watching weirdly cheerful presenters on CBeebies at 6.30 a.m. on a Saturday morning. So here's the deal, child-free people at work: try not to discuss your weekend plans in front of colleagues with kids. We already hate your guts. There's no need to make it worse.

The Phone Call

Is it okay to return a friend's call three days after he phones you? Yes, everything is possible once you have kids.

'Hi, sorry I'm only getting back to you now. I was going to call you back Tuesday, but Jack managed to vomit out his ass. Then he hid my phone in the oven.'

'Could you not ring it from the landline?'

'I had it on silent, because I didn't want it to wake Jack during the night.'

'I hear that happens a lot.'

'I couldn't ring yesterday because I was actually too tired to talk about football and the fastest way to get from Cork to Sligo. It's come to that. Why were you ringing me anyway?'

'My wife is pregnant again.'

'Sorry to hear that. See you in three years' time so.'

'Yeah.'

Nothing, I'm Grand

Irish people hate it when you refuse a drink:

'My round, what are you having?'

'Nothing, I'm grand.'

'Do you mind going home so, you're making the rest of us feel like alcoholics.'

That's why you never refuse a drink. And then baby comes along. That's not a third glass of wine you are being offered. It's the seventh circle of hell. It's you, your hangover and a bawling baby sitting on the living-room floor at 8.30 a.m. the next morning. It's the longest day of your life. It's why it's perfectly okay to say, 'Nothing, I'm grand' on a night out. But make sure to hang around for an hour or two, just to make your friends feel uncomfortable about their drinking. Take that, you people with an actual life!

Say Yes to Shopping. Really.

Before he becomes a father, your average man is more likely to treat himself to a box set of *Grey's Anatomy*, than he is to visit a shopping centre. Unless he is brought there by his partner so she can accidentally on purpose point out what she'd like for Christmas. That's a trip no man wants to miss.

A man who buys the correct present three years in a row is now in a position to ask the woman to marry him. All going well, they'll have kids. And once kids are on the scene he'll never want to go anywhere else other than a shopping centre. The safe, open spaces. The encouraging sight of other parents barely managing to control their kids. It's like heaven, but with Starbucks, McDonald's and Pick 'n' Mix. Embrace the shopping centre, Dad, it's impossible to live without it.

The Magic Roundabout

Here's one thing we know about a man who drives around a roundabout twice, before going on his way. He has at least one child in a car seat in the back. And that's why he's in no rush to go home. Your car changes once you have a child. No longer is it a way to get from A to B, or ram your creditworthiness down everyone else's throat. (The Credit Union – where 'home improvement' on the application form can sometimes mean a new Hyundai.)

Once you have kids, the car becomes a place you can legally

restrain them for hours on end. Nice. So, here's a tip when you are going out for a drive. Maybe wear a nappy yourself. It would be a shame to have to come home early just because you have to use the jacks.

Say Yes to Drugs

There was a time you'd avoid someone who kept banging on about their favourite drugs. And worry about them if they couldn't pass a bottle without giving it a hug.

That all changes when you have kids. Suddenly there are only two words that matter. Calpol and Nurofen. Those two wonder-drugs are the key to child-rearing these days, now that you're not really allowed to get them all goosed up on Dozol. As for putting a drop of brandy in the bottle, I'd keep that to myself if I were you. Maybe in the future people will frown on how we eased our kids through the early years with Calpol and Nurofen. But for now they are your best friends in the whole wide world.

2.11 DEALING WITH DROWSY

It's okay, you're not going to puke. That's just tiredness. There was a year after our second child came along, when we were woken up at least once a night. That was when the bouts of nausea started. I can remember sitting on the couch wondering if I had enough energy to run to the toilet. (I hadn't, really.) I never actually puked, it would pass, or I would close my eyes and nap for a while, with that lovely tingling sensation I get at the top of my ears when I'm drifting off to sleep.

These naps never ended well. If I was lucky, a child would

crawl or walk in and start poking at my eyes. The alternative ending was when my wife caught me trying to have a sneaky nap. That usually involved a list of things I could have been doing if I wasn't having a sleep.

I don't blame her; I'm the same. For all the determination to work at this together, there is something incredibly selfish about your desire to sleep. Here's a run-through of some of my coping mechanisms.

Coffee

Parenting is mainly about looking forward to your next cup of coffee. This is the one that's going to save the day, says you, hoping against hope. And sometimes it works. One minute you're wondering if it's possible to put your kids up on eBay. Three sips of espresso later and you suddenly feel something approaching affection for the little mites. Two more sips and you've upgraded that feeling to full-on love. What could possibly go wrong?

Everything. You know nothing about despair until you have experienced a coffee hangover. This is where you lose the run of yourself and have two double espressos in a row. Ten minutes later you have a weird feeling you are going to puke out through your toes. Ten minutes after that you pay a visit to the toilet that registers on the Richter Scale. In China. So, keep it to two coffees a day, at least four hours apart. And if you're anything like me, don't touch caffeine after 2 p.m. Unless you plan to counteract it with a spot of booze, in which case you'll stay up drinking longer and then sleep like the baby that wakes you three hours after you went to bed. Try to picture that before you order that late-night espresso.

Go to Bed

Sorry for being so obvious. But first-time parents often resist going to bed at 9 p.m. because it makes them feel old. Here is how that pans out. You stick with an 11 p.m. bedtime for three months. At which point you take stock of your face in the mirror. You look seventy-five years of age. (Not good, unless you are in fact seventy-five, in which case, hello, Mick Jagger and thanks for reading.)

Here's the lowdown, Dad. Go to bed at 9 p.m. There is an outside chance you will feel up for a quickie and manage to guilt herself into doing it before she falls asleep. Or, failing that, make the case that a quickie will help her get to sleep. If you reckon wrecked parents have sex for a reason other than guilt and 'it will help you sleep', then I have some bad news for you.

Game of Snores

Here's how things worked for your parents. There was nothing good on telly after 10 p.m., so they went to bed and made your baby brother. It's much harder to drag yourself off the couch these days. This is because of what people call box sets, even though we all know it is in fact a dodgy android box you bought off Dave at work. (Not his real name. The whole thing is very dodgy.)

These 'box sets' are usually put on ten minutes after the last cry from the cot and left on until one of you can't focus on the screen. They are bad news on the sleep front, as you end up going to bed shortly before Chloe wakes up. And an army of the dead from *Game of Thrones* has nothing on Chloe when you have only had three hours' sleep. So, here's the golden rule for 'box sets' – two episodes, then bed.

Wine O'Clock

You are probably familiar with Wine O'Clock. This is the point of the evening when you can start drinking wine without people saying you're an alcoholic. Some parents swear by it as a means to unwind and get to sleep.

In case you are wondering, Wine O'Clock in Ireland is 7 p.m. on a Tuesday, because if you start back on the booze on a Monday your family might stage an intervention. (That's not all bad – while they're all there you should be able to strong-arm one of them into taking the kids, so you can both go to Palma for a long weekend. Loads of booze in Palma.)

Here is another important time for new parents who plan to cut loose at Wine O'Clock. It's called Whine O'Clock. That's where little Jack wakes up at 6 a.m. and starts whining about a lost teddy or some other catastrophe. You only realise you have a hangover when you hear him shouting, 'I won't mention Teddy again Dad, just unlock the door and let me out of the hot-press.' Whine O'Clock is never worth it. So go for a one glass maximum at Wine O'Clock.

Show Me a Sign

There's no easy way to put this – kids give you early onset dementia. Here is how it manifests itself. It's yet another morning after a sleepless night. You find yourself standing in a random room with no idea why you went in there. In an attempt to maintain their dignity, some parents will pick up a random item and pretend that's what they were looking for all along. It's why, when you call over to see people with small kids, you'll often find one parent rambling around the house with a packet of wipes, a onesie and a toilet brush.

There isn't a whole lot of dignity in that. So here's my advice, Dads, because you are the ones being sent around to get stuff. The trick is to place memory jolt posters in appropriate rooms. So, for example, put 'It's probably a thermometer' by the medicine cabinet. And in the kid's bedroom, try 'Bring back a onesie, vest, socks, nappy, indoor hat, outdoor hat and pick up a treat-size pack of Maltesers in the kitchen for herself. That should cover it.'

The Power Nap

The best thing about being a man is you are genetically programmed to take a power nap. Some say this is because we had to reboot ourselves when we were out on a hunt, but really, it's just because we're lazy. Anyway, you'd be amazed how ten minutes of kip can change your day. Not that you'll ever get to find out. Unless you can sleep through your partner going, 'Are you for real? And don't be giving me that bullshit about hunting with your cavemen friends.'

The message here is simple. Don't try this at home. Volunteer for any job that involves driving and grab ten minutes in the car park by Aldi. Or more, if there's a match on the radio.

Chocolate

Research shows that 98% of chocolate sales are driven by parents trying to fill the gap where their life used to be. It also tends to fill a gap around where their abs used to be, but that's only half the problem. The real issue is that a well-earned chocolate reward at 8 p.m. turns into a staring at the ceiling problem at 3 a.m. And it's also a substitute for sex, so you don't even feel like waking your partner to 'discuss' your issues. Not that any guy would seriously consider interrupting his partner's sleep. Unless you are doing research for a movie called *SheWolf 7 – This Time You Might Never Hear the End of It*.

Escape to the Attic?

'There is no point in both of us being wrecked.' You'll often hear parents of newborns saying this, explaining why one of them (usually Dad) sleeps in the spare room or attic.

This is a good idea, as long as you are the one dozing through the madness. And that only lasts until your partner somehow gets ten minutes' sleep and the part of her brain marked 'he's taking the piss' will flicker into action. So here's my advice. Get out of the attic and back into bed. Because there is actually a point in both of you being wrecked. The point being you could spend the next eleven years paying her back with random acts of kindness.

Joking aside, there are times where there is no point in both of you lying awake in the same bed, particularly if your partner is breastfeeding through the night. So plan ahead, with a spare room as far away as possible. There is something else you should plan ahead for while you are at it. And that's the resentment that will build up when one partner is getting more sleep than the other. Don't lie awake in the spare room worrying about it. Get some kip and make sure you offer your partner her own nap-time the following day.

ASMR Sleep Whisperers

A lot of people swear by these ASMR* sleep apps, where you listen to a woman with a soothing voice telling you to go to sleep. It isn't kinky as such, unless you are the sort that gets turned on by a video of a whispering lady, pretending to brush your hair. (They probably make you pay extra at the barbers.) That said, search for ASMR on YouTube and you will end up watching a clip of a whispering English woman pretending to be a travel agent in what is clearly her bedroom. It's not something you want to get caught doing by your partner, even if it does help your sleep.

* ASMR stands for Autonomous Sensory Meridian Response. I doubt that's made it any clearer. Have a look at some apps on YouTube and see what you think.

2.12 MIND YOUR MIND – DAD'S MENTAL HEALTH

They called it a nervous breakdown when I was growing up. My mother would tell us that so-and-so had one, whispering the words 'nervous breakdown' in case she caught it herself. This 'disease' was anything that didn't show up in an X-ray and covered the whole spectrum of mental illness. The less said about it, the better.

Now there is no shortage of famous people coming out to talk about their struggles with depression, anxiety, post-traumatic stress disorder and various other conditions. This openness is a good thing, even though sometimes it can feel like you need one of these conditions just to get on TV.

But you still don't hear much about the effect of fatherhood on your mental health. Women are rightly encouraged to watch out for signs of post-natal depression and seek help if they need it. Men, not so much. It's almost like we couldn't be affected because we didn't push out the child. And anyway, our job is to say nothing and plough on, like our fathers did.

This doesn't tally with what dads tell me in private. A friend of mine said being a father to small kids was up there with the Leaving Cert as one of the most traumatic and stressful periods of his life. Others have said something similar, in hushed tones, because we're not supposed to find it tough.

Guess what? It's tough. Having a child is guaranteed to put a strain on your mental well-being. The world as you know it falls apart once there's a new baby in the house. Sleep is a goner for a while, you see too little of your friends and too much of your partner (and don't worry, she feels the same way about you).

This doesn't mean every man is bound for a breakdown. But if you don't actively look after your mental health when the kids are under four, I think there is a chance you could end up overwhelmed. If you feel it's all too much, tell your partner and go seek some help.

I'm no expert. All I know is that these are some of the things that helped me to forget potties and Calpol for a while, and blow off some steam.

Date a Dad

It used to be five-a-side soccer, before my ankles staged an intervention and said you're probably not going to play for Manchester United now, what with being forty-five and useless. I felt that was a bit harsh, but there is no point in ignoring your joints once you hit middle age. So now I play squash. It's a once a week affair with another dad. We talk about our kids on the drive to the squash club, he always wins the game because he's younger than me and probably trains on the sly, we always say we must go out for a pint some time, but never do. The next day he Vibers me a graph of his heart-rate to show how much energy we used. We both agree we must do it again the following week and we do.

This has nothing to do with getting good at squash. (Trust me on that one.) It's just something vaguely competitive we can do, in all weathers, to blow away the minor irks and cobwebs that build up when there are kids in your life. It's better than a gym session, because neither of us feel we can back out at the last minute in case we let the other guy down. That matters when the couch is pretty much saying, 'Why don't you just sit down here with a sharing pack of Maltesers and binge-watch *Breaking Bad*?' (If your couch does actually start talking to you, that might be a good time to seek help.)

Date Your Partner

My wife has put an embargo on discussing our private life in public, and who could blame her? That said, I have a friend who swears by a bit of sex. He says that it changes the mood at home and takes the edge off his stress levels. But he also said you can't just expect your partner to get 'em off as a tonic for your mental well-being – you both need to get out on a date more often, so you can reconnect as a couple.

This is important, because women find it hard to have sex when there is a distance between them and their partner, according to my friend. So it might be a good idea to go on a few dates with your partner. As long as you don't keep checking your watch to see how long before you can go home and have sex. That can be a bit off-putting, apparently.

I'd recommend an Italian restaurant if you are on an overnight stay with your partner, in a hotel, away from the kids. I'd also recommend you order the spaghetti Bolognese. Do you know what it tastes like when the sauce isn't being used to disguise two blended sweet potatoes, eighty-seven carrots and a head of cabbage? Spaghetti Bolognese, that's what it tastes like. While you're at it, order and eat all the desserts at your leisure. You'd be amazed how good tiramisu is when you are not ramming it down your throat because the babysitter costs double after midnight.

A word of warning here – your date might not go to plan. You wouldn't believe the pressure on a couple with young kids for this to be THE BEST DATE OF ALL TIME. You might even bring the voiceover guy from *X Factor*, so he can give it a sense of occasion: Ladies and Gentlemen, please welcome Pat and Rose, they are taking a night off from their two toddlers! Oh look, THEY ARE BOTH ASLEEP ON THE TABLE.

Face the Music

It started as an assignment from a newspaper. They wanted me to try something out of my comfort zone for six weeks and write about it. Someone suggested joining an African Drumming class. That was so far outside my comfort zone, I reckoned I'd be lucky to last a fortnight. I really had no interest in getting in touch with my inner African.

Two years later and I'm still doing it once a week. It's not just that I love the drums. What worked for me was that I took on something completely new when the kids came along, something that was just for me. What worked for my wife is this doesn't involve hang-gliding or climbing Everest, so she won't be left to raise the kids by herself.

We play rhythms which are used to drive out evil spirits and bad juju in West Africa. I don't want to put anyone off having kids, but you are pretty much guaranteed bad juju in a house where no one is getting any sleep. I never thought I'd admit this in public, but I think banging a goat skin for ninety minutes a week with some strangers helps clear the air around me. My friend who has taken up guitar says the same. So, pick up an instrument and give it a go.

Stick with the Booze

I don't want to be flippant about alcohol, given the link between substance abuse and self-harm or suicide. But I love a drink. There was a time when I loved it too well and was probably drinking too much. Now, I genuinely think I might be drinking too little. This happens to a lot of casual drinkers when the kids come along. You stick with the bottle of wine for a few Friday nights, until you notice that Saturdays seem to last for thirty-seven hours and you're fit to cry at 10 a.m. It's just not worth the hangover.

Worse again, if your partner is pregnant or breastfeeding, you're down a drinking buddy. (It's great she's pregnant obviously, but you'd miss her all the same.) As a result, I pretty much stopped drinking altogether and ended up a mess whenever I did manage a few pints with my friends.

I replaced booze with tea. But it isn't really Friday night when you're sitting down with a mug of camomile. There was nothing to mark the end of the week and it felt like I was stuck in a rut. That's when I discovered the top shelf in my supermarket off-licence, with decent wines for about fifteen quid. Two glasses of red on a Friday night, with a posh packet of crisps, won't give me a hangover. But it's enough to feel like a reward at the end of the week.

Better still, it's enough to stop me slurring like an amateur when I go out for a few pints.

Best of all, it allows me to laugh out loud at *Gogglebox* or whatever else passes for comedy on Friday night. I've watched those shows with nothing stronger than camomile tea coursing through my veins and they're not half as funny as people think they are.

Don't Mind Mindfulness

Mindfulness is still all the rage as I write. It's a philosophy that maintains you should be present in every moment and stop worrying about the future. Here's one thing we can say about the people who came up with mindfulness. They don't have kids. Or, if they do, their kids are the boy who arrives in school carrying a Yorkie for lunch and wearing his sister's tights. The only people happy with that arrangement are

Nestlé. (The little boy would probably be okay with it, if it wasn't for the tights.)

Sorry, but the last thing you can do as a parent is stop thinking about what's coming next. Unless it's 9 p.m. and they are finally all in bed. And you have all the lunches ready. And dinners made three months in advance. And you remembered to ring your mother back because you missed her call. And you have just given the house a lick of paint.

The life of a parent can be very tough if you don't keep on top of things. So, in short, I'd leave mindfulness to people who have nothing better to do with their time.

Phone a Friend

I know it's virtually illegal these days to imply there is a difference between the sexes, but sometimes you just need to talk to a man. This can be tricky with a small kid around, when you end up cut off from your friends, in what people call the baby tunnel. It's doubly tricky for me because I work from home.

Men aren't great at keeping in touch with their friends and I'm no exception. But one thing my friends and I do is to put a date in the diary and head away for the weekend. (Tell your partner before you go, it can look a bit sloppy if you just walk out the door.)

The last one I did was a short weekend in Dingle, which involved a long hike, pints and pizzas. We all agreed it was great to get away from our kids, then spent the next forty-eight hours talking about them.

One final tip here. Stay off Facebook whenever possible. And not just because it's a bad idea to stare at your phone every night before going to bed. The problem with over-sharing on Facebook is there's nothing to tell your friends when you meet up in the flesh. (And, there's a good chance they'll think you're a loser for posting twice a day.) You're far better off to keep your best stories and photos for the trip away.

Try a Makeover

Looked in the mirror recently? Dressing like your dad? That's a shortcut to feeling old and bad about yourself. It's time for you to buy something new and youthful.

Just not too youthful. If there is the slightest hint of Justin Bieber, hand the clothes back to the lady in the shop and walk straight out the door. Seriously, the slagging when you go away with your mates isn't worth it.

Still, there is nothing like a bit of sprucing up to get your mojo back. I like buying new clothes, it's a handy slice of me time, and it's nice to be able to put on a pair of jeans in the changing room without a small person pointing and asking, 'What's that, Dad?'

Never bring them into the changing room, by the way. That's your sacred space and I'd be the last to judge if you decided to lie down on the ground and grab 30 minutes' kip.

Five Things that just Add to the Stress

1: **Working from home.** You mightn't have a choice in this. If you do work from home, make sure you get out for a walk or meet someone for coffee every other day. Because cabin fever should be classed as a medical condition.

2: **Late-night chocolate.** Yes, you deserve a second bar of chocolate watching *Breaking Bad*. No, you won't be able to get to sleep until 4 a.m.

3: **Going with the flow.** There's nothing more stressful than taking it easy on a lazy Saturday afternoon. Children need entertainment, always make a plan.

4: **Broccoli.** Did you eat broccoli when you were young? No? Then why are you trying to force-feed it to your kids?

5: **An Affair.** I presume I don't have to tell you why this is a bad idea. And not just because you'll be too tired to keep it a secret.

3

THE TERRIBLE TWOS

Times have changed since Irish men 'visited' their wives in the labour ward so they could get started on baby number two. Okay, maybe this never happened, but you know what I mean. The Irish twins phenomenon – where there is a ten-month gap between siblings – does seem like a thing of the past. So there is a good chance you'll enter the third year of fatherhood with only one child.

That's a good thing. You should be allowed time to enjoy your two-year-old. Forget all the terrible twos talk – my cousin was right when she told me not to worry about that, because toddlers are magic. That's the age when they start to emerge and find the words to tell you what they've been thinking since they were born.

I'm not saying two is a breeze. It's also the age when they start to fully appreciate the power of the word 'no' and the benefits of acting stroppy in public. It can be a big adjustment from the placid baby years. Here is what I made of it, starting with a brief dummy's guide to toddlers.

3.1 TODDLER SURVIVAL GUIDE
The Terrible Twos. And Threes.
They call it the Terrible Twos. That's misleading on a couple of counts. First of all, it usually lasts until they are four.

You'll probably be told that by a so-called friend, after the first tantrum. Ah fantastic, and there was I thinking we'd be through this in a year. 'Actually, my fella stayed crazy until he was about six,' says another friend, improving matters no end.

The other problem? Two-year-olds aren't terrible all of the time. Just when you start wondering if there is some kind of warranty programme where you can return them to the hospital, they sing every last word of *Itsy Bitsy Spider* and turn you into a ball of mush. That's what you are up against here. That's how devious they are.

It Will Pass

Some tantrums will make you worry that your child is carrying the seed of the devil. But that still isn't the worst thing. No, the real problem with tantrums is contained in three words – it will pass.

It's the kind of thing you hear from old ladies on the bus, as your toddler does his nut. There are two responses to this. A: You can smile in gratitude, or B: You can scream, 'When exactly will it pass, you crazy old bag who doesn't have to share a house with a two-foot-tall terrorist?'

Go for option A. Shouting at old ladies on the bus is never a good look. People will just turn to each other and say, 'You can see where the poor child gets it from.' And you'll be back to worrying about the whole seed of the devil thing.

The Problem with Restaurants

You might not be familiar with Toddler Time. That's the game other diners play when you bring your two-year-old into a restaurant. Everyone tries to guess how long before you call a waiter over and say, 'Please just give me the bill, my toddler has gone nuts.' So now you know why that guy at the next table stood up and shouted, 'Yes!'

Here's the problem. A lot of kids make the transition from infant to toddler in a crowded restaurant. They go in as adorable babies. They come out roaring their purple little heads off, as their parents google 'Exorcisms R Us'. So here's my advice. Eat at home for a few months. It's the new going out for people with two-year-olds. Otherwise you're just fodder for the Toddler Time crowd.

Vengeance

Toddlers. Can't take them out in public; can't stay cooped up with them for more than seven minutes. Don't worry, there is a middle ground. You can always visit the people who visited you with their toddlers.

It's pay-back time. You're back, and this time you're packing your own toddler. Watch their faces fall when they realise the shoe is on the other foot. Relax for an hour, let someone else worry if your Jack is going to get his head stuck in the dog. It's revenge for the times she turned up at your door with her Rory and the snot that hung all the way down to his knee.

There is only one golden rule for the vengeance visit. Never ring ahead. You can't afford to lose the element of surprise.

Meet Your Baby Brother

You'll have heard the golden rule about dealing with a toddler

– don't poke the tiger. Sorry for being so crude, but a better tip is don't poke the missus.

Because let's just say toddlers aren't great at sharing attention. Here's what you should do to make sure your toddler is okay with a baby sibling. Nothing. Seriously, it's all a waste of time. They say you should give your toddler a present from his new sibling to help him cope. Well, 'they' own toy companies. Here is how that present registered in the toddler's mind. 'I got a new sister and a new Cookie Monster. I'm going to keep the Cookie Monster.'

Sugar, Daddy?

Bad news, guys. Your child isn't saying 'Dada' because he prefers you to Mom. It's just his first attempt to say, 'I love Maltesers. You can give me some now. Or later. Just bear in mind that I'll really enjoy the tantrum that comes in between.'

Toddlers are always on the hunt for the next sugar hit. Our two-year-old dispensed with 'good morning' in favour of 'another rice cake?' (That's a rice cake with what they call a yogurt topping, but come on, we all know it's chocolate.) Naturally we didn't give her one. Until after 10 a.m. We're all about the strict parenting in our place.

The Art of Bribery

The outside world can be a scary place. At some point in your travels, your child will decide they both want to stay put and go home at exactly the same time. If you think a toddler will make this clear in their inside-the-house voice, then you haven't been paying attention.

So now you're in a busy shopping centre, trying to figure out how to manipulate the space-time continuum, while your child does his nut. As I said, there is every chance that a stranger will stop to tell you not to worry, this will pass. There are only two things that might work here. A chocolate bribe for your crazy child, followed by a different chocolate bribe because, let's face it, he won't like the first one. Never leave home without both of them.

Mind Your Language

Some things are certain with a toddler in the house.

1: Your cursing will increase by at least 40%.

2: So will your toddler's. Two-year-olds are like parrots. Or as they say themselves, 'fucking parrots'.

3: You will pretend to be appalled when they say 'fucking hell' for the first time, even though you are secretly thrilled. Ah look, he's just like me.

4: You try the 'Aren't they gas at that age?' approach when your two-year-old calls the public health nurse a nosey bitch. It doesn't work. There's a certain tension during her subsequent visits.

5: Your toddler brings back a few new curses she learned in the crèche. They grow up so quickly, the little shaggers.

Not Old Enough, Not Yet

There is a temptation to think that just because they are sharp and manipulative, toddlers should be able to dress themselves. That would be a mistake.

Watching a two-year-old boy dressing himself is like looking at a man wearing gloves, trying to wind his watch. It's impossible to stay focused on your own task and not intervene. (Unless you think it's possible to stir porridge when a toddler stumbles into the kitchen with his head in his underpants. That's my boy, says you, vaguely remembering parts of your stag party.)

Your kids might learn to dress themselves over time. But you won't be there to witness it. Instead you'll be locked up in a high-security facility, muttering 'That sleeve is inside out, try again' to yourself all day long.

Here's my advice. There is no rush – keep dressing them yourself until they are three, going on four.

3.2 HOW'S YOUR CHRISTMAS?

Just because it's a cliché doesn't mean it's untrue – kids make your Christmas all over again. The reason I talk about it here, in the Terrible Twos section, is because while your child's first Christmas is important to you and your partner, all the kid can see is lots of stress and slightly more toys than usual. (Kids get toys all year round now, mainly made by kids their own age in China. You can try and fight this if you like, but there is nothing to be done about aunts and uncles who can't resist an Action Man in Dealz for €2.50.) The real fun starts when they are around two years' old and can appreciate what's going on.

Here's what you need to watch out for in the run-up to Christmas.

The Santa Experience

Gone are the days when kids would line up to get a lucky bag from 'Santa' or, as he was better known, Eddie from the Credit Union. Now they have to have an 'Experience'. It might also be called a 'Journey', if the person running it watches too much *X Factor*. You might be inclined to call it a 'Rip-Off'.

The 'Journey' takes about an hour, although it seems longer. Most of it involves watching your kids being shouted at by over-excited teenagers dressed as elves. Then it's on to Santa's cave, where there are a lot of tears, mainly yours when you see the crap present you got for fifteen euro. Try not to ask why parents have to pay for the 'Journey' as well. This will only upset Santa and you don't want to get on the wrong side of him at this time of year.

The Toy Run

10.37 a.m. on a Monday morning in early December. This is what you calculate as the best time to go your local toy superstore. The kids will be in school. The school-drop parents will have come and gone. You clear everything out of the boot. The entire Santa run done and dusted in an hour. This is going to be so cool.

10.37 a.m. on a Monday morning in early December. The time every other parent in a forty-kilometre radius has calculated is the best time to go to their local toy superstore. The traffic jam is so bad that it makes the six o'clock news. In Los Angeles. You know what to do. Wait until Christmas Eve. Nobody ever thinks of going then. (Not a guarantee. And I take no responsibility for the availability of that must-have doll. Or that you might end up as the first parents in Ireland to be divorced by their little girl.)

The Dancing Santa

It was so funny in the shop that you bought two. A cheap Santa that dances around to perky Hungarian dance music – what's not to like? Perky Hungarian dance music, as it turns out. Never underestimate a toddler's ability to listen to the same song 873 squillion times in a row.

The UN moved to stop prisoners in Guantanamo Bay being tortured by the theme tune from *Barney & Friends*. You'd think they could do something for you in your own home. You'd think wrong. There's only one solution. Fake a burglary in your own house by a dangerous gang of Santa lovers.

All being well, you should finally be able to stop humming perky Hungarian dance music in time for Easter. If you are lucky.

The Auntie Problem

Your sister calls on the phone. 'I was thinking of getting your little Sophie a pair of pink Doc Martens with a searchlight out of the front of them. What do you think?'

Here's something you know, deep down. Your sister has already bought the Docs and is fantasising about Sophie wearing them to your parents' place on Christmas Day. Telling her what you actually think of a two-year-old in a pair of Docs means Sophie will grow up without ever really knowing her aunt.

So here is how you need to reply. 'I hate you so much. I was going to get her those. You are the Queen of buying presents.'

The Hangover

Ah go on, it's Christmas, says you, opening the third bottle of wine. Apparently, some couples go the whole hog and have actual sex. (Sure it's only once a year.)

It's office party time as well, where one of you goes out on the mojitos, safe in the knowledge that the other one will take care of the kids the following day. This isn't as clever as it sounds. Unless you enjoy lying hungover on the couch while your partner scuttles around muttering, 'Isn't it well for some.' (It's a buzz-wrecker.)

Here's what I reckon. Christmas won't work unless both of you have exactly the same hangover. So, if your partner is out with her work crowd, it might be an idea to have a few sneaky scoops at home. Okay, your kid will have pizza for breakfast, lunch and dinner the next day. But look at it this way – they're hardly going to complain.

Beware the Stollen

The good thing about Halloween is that it only gives you a two-month run-in to Christmas. Think of all the extra tins of Roses you might have eaten if they moved it back to mid-October. You'd be like a medium-sized Texan.

Mind you, there is a chance to get up to that size if the supermarkets get their way. The main culprit here is stollen, the ridiculously addictive dried fruit and marzipan cake they have all over Aldi and Lidl. It's particularly addictive when you have young kids and need a tasty sugar-hit.

We tend to view it as health-food because it comes from Germany. The Germans themselves see it as a cake. Research shows that the average Irish person eats one whole stollen a day, in the five weeks leading up to Christmas.* This can rise to two Stollens if you eat the handy bite-sized ones. (As in, they are a handy revenue boost for people who manufacture XXXXXL-size action-slacks.)

So here is your final tip for a happy Christmas. Step away from the stollen. (You are probably unable to run at this stage.)

* Not quite made up. It is true, based on research I carried out on myself.

Okay, so you've made it through the run-up to Christmas Day, possibly hungover and a little overweight. That's when the fun really kicks off. Here is a typical timetable:

Christmas Eve, 10.30 p.m. Don't exchange gifts with your partner on Christmas Eve. This was cool and often ended in living-room sex back before the kids came along and used up all your money. Now you're exchanging bargain perfume and leather gloves. This has the same effect on your sex drive as watching an episode of *One Born Every Minute*. You'll end up going to bed worried that the fizz has gone out of your relationship. Wait until the morning for the pressie business, when the kids' enthusiasm will put a gloss on everything. If that doesn't work, crack open the first bottle of Prosecco. Gloves! Wow, honey, I love you so much. I love everything so much.

Christmas Morning, 4 a.m. Don't go in and force the kids to get up and look at their presents. It isn't their fault you have a weird obsession with Santa and tend to get over-excited at Christmas time. Or that you ate a tin of Roses last night and probably won't sleep again until January. If you are really looking for something to do, get up and put the turkey on. It's never too early. Don't mind Jamie Oliver, trying to poison us all with a turkey that was only cooked for five hours. Jamie just doesn't get that it wouldn't be Christmas time in Ireland if we didn't have turkey that is drier than the Gobi Desert.

7 a.m. The kids are up and the presents are open. There is just one problem. And no, it isn't a lack of batteries. You've been burned on that front before and have enough AA and AAA batteries this year to run the LUAS. The problem is the microscopic screw on the cover of the battery compartment. You try to open it with your smallest screwdriver. Nothing happens, except this Christmas will be remembered as the year your toddler learned the C word. (It's all about making memories.)

You end up googling 'opticians open Christmas Day' because, in truth, you can't see what you are doing. So here's my advice. When you are out buying batteries for Christmas, pick up an extra-small screwdriver as well. And maybe go to Specsavers.

11 a.m. The real problem with a two-year-old? They can't tell you what they want for Christmas. So you buy a retro rocking-horse because who doesn't like a retro rocking-horse? Well, your two-year-old as it turns out. He has just climbed into the box for your four-year-old's doll's house and pulled the lid down on top of him. This should be the cutest thing of all time but you secretly despise him for not sharing your love of retro rocking-horses. You pour a fresh glass of Prosecco and start to love him again. Aaaaw. How did people cope before bubbles for breakfast on Christmas morning?

Two take-aways here. Two-year-olds don't get retro. And under no circumstances should you run out of Prosecco.

2 p.m. The boiled spuds are ready for mashing. Just get the gravy done and the kids can be fed. Except you can't deglaze the roasting tin because the turkey is stuck to the bottom of it. You let rip with some curses you learned from a Quentin Tarantino movie just as your grand-aunt walks into the kitchen. At least she'll have something to tell the other nuns when she goes back to the convent later.

You take the roast carrots out of the oven but there is no worktop space to put them down. You decide to put them back in the oven but there is no room for them there either. How the fuck did that happen? And now your Prosecco has gone warm. And your two-year-old turned up the oven so your roasties look like coal. Worst of all, you allowed the kids to drink Coke for the first time this morning and now they have toddler hangovers. The take-away here? A large roast chicken for the adults, pizza for the kids. Now that's a Happy Christmas.

3 p.m. That glorious period when everyone is fed and the kids are still interested in their toys. This is what Christmas is all about.

3.10 p.m. The kids lose interest in their toys. Possibly because they are already broken. You notice that toys featuring either a queen who turns things to ice, or a pass-remarkable little pig with a brother called George are usually the first to go wonky. The take-away here? There isn't one. Sorry about that. Large corporations will make tacky crap off the back of a movie and you will buy it at a 5,000% mark-up. This is also what Christmas is all about.

5 p.m. The kitchen is cleared up so you can finally get back to that tin of Roses. It's time for the greatest Christmas tradition of them all – agreeing that there is nothing on the telly. You turn on *EastEnders* that you recorded from earlier. It's impossible to feel goodwill towards your fellow humans while watching one drunk cockney screaming at another one. (This is one area where even Prosecco doesn't work.)

So you start flicking through the channels, until you get to *Chitty Chitty Bang Bang* on ITV4+1. Brilliant, your kids don't say at all. Five minutes later you are all watching *Twirlywoos* on YouTube. It isn't *Willy Wonka* or *The Sound of Music*. But it is the first time today they cuddled into you under a blanket in front of the fire. The take-away here? It's only once a year for a few years. So enjoy it while you can.

3.3 SPRING CLEANING IN JANUARY

Why January? Because it's after Christmas. Tidying up is a big part of your life all year round, but it steps up a gear after Christmas because the house is extra full of crap. So while this advice comes into its own in the early week of a new year, it can apply anytime really.

Tidying up is not to be confused with housework, which I dealt with earlier in the book. Housework is anything that needs to be done at a particular time to make sure the whole family operation keeps ticking over.

Tidying up is about pretending to pick stuff up off the floor and then throwing 80% of it in the bin, because the kids won't miss it. (Never let a child look in your recycling bin. They're very attached to things they forgot they owned.)

Trust me, if you have a problem with clutter, you're going to have problems with kids. Particularly when they get to the age of two and have the concentration span of a goldfish. The net result is that they will have ten toys, jigsaws, doll's houses, bears and mice on the floor at any one time, along with 15,000 small pieces of plastic. That can rise to 30,000 once all the Christmas presents have been opened and flung across the floor. Here's a run-through of what you can expect.

The Floor of Death

Ah Christmas, that special time when toys seem to fall apart after ten minutes. Add in an army of aunties who can't decide which of the cheap gizmos to buy at the queue in Penneys, so they buy them all. The result? By early January the floor in your place is a sea of doll-heads and wheels.

Stoop down for a look and you'll end up kneeling on some fake Lego. This is more painful than being eaten by a shark, but you're a man and not allowed to talk about pain ever again. (You had the 'flu' over Christmas and overdid it on the moaning front. It's okay, we all do that.) The solution? Hire one of those industrial vacuum cleaners and clear the floor in half an hour. The crunching sound is immensely satisfying. And there is no way the kids can miss all of it.

The Bike

Face it. Your daughter didn't want a bike. There was no way of knowing this before Christmas. Didn't she hug it in the toy shop and everything, and even gave it a name? The problem wasn't really with the bike. The problem is you bought a

Frozen dress in Aldi on Christmas Eve, just in case. Anyway, she's worn the dress for fifteen days solid since Christmas and won't go near her main present because Ice Queens don't have time for cycling. (It's obvious when you think about it.) So now you have to squeeze the bike into your chaotic shed. Which is a balls, because you were hoping you wouldn't have to face into shed-clearing until March at the earliest. There's another weekend gone.

The Wardrobe

The problem with cleaning up isn't knowing when to start. It's knowing when to stop. What starts out as an attempt to rationalise the toy situation ends up with your wife in your bedroom shouting, 'Do you really need seven shirts?' The correct response to this is, 'No, throw out whatever you want.' Unfortunately, you have given up chocolate for January and are therefore mad for a fight. So you shout, 'About as much as you need eighteen tops that don't really fit you any more.'

Jesus, what were you thinking? It started out as an attempt to clear the front room. It ended up in family court. The take-away here is straightforward. A tidy-up row can escalate very quickly, so make sure both of you have a strong coffee before you start. At least then you'll be in a good mood for a couple of hours.

The Attic

The main thing you need to throw out for a tidy house? The pull-down stairs for your attic. Why? The First Law of Keeping Stuff Forever. It states that the amount of garbage in your gaff is directly proportional to the quality of access to your attic. Put another way, it's hard to drag an old lawnmower up a rickety ladder. You want to make it harder, not easier, to keep stuff.

Now, like most men, you probably harbour notions of disappearing up to the attic for the weekend to watch illegal streams of soccer matches on that Android TV box you bought from Dodgy Dave. However, it's hard to escape into your man-mind when surrounded by boxes of old onesies, kept in case you decide to have another child. So, throw out those stairs and seal up the attic.

The Books

Your kids probably got loads of new books for Christmas. Just as well. There aren't any surprises left in *The Gruffalo* after reading it 1,142 times. (*The Gruffalo*? Why, didn't you know? It's a charming book that goes like so.)

Anyway, this is an ideal time to clear out some old books. So you and the missus sit down and start going through the pile. (Rule One of tidying up. Never dump anything without written permission.) The net result is you end up throwing out no books. Zero. Not even the one about the fox and the butterfly that reads like it was translated from Chinese by a four-year-old Portuguese hamster. You see, it still has that bit of Sophie's puke on page three. You can still kind of smell it if you stick your nose right in. Aaaw. You end up buying a new bookcase instead.

The Storage Boxes

Damn you, big supermarket chains. First you trick us into buying a ton of toys that our kids don't want, by luring us into your shop with gorgeous wine at amazing prices. Knowing how this pans out, you greet the new year with mounds of storage boxes on special offer, for these freshly unloved toys. So now our house is ceiling high with empty storage boxes. We're too sad to fill them up with rubbish, because we gave up your gorgeous wine for January. The upshot is we need a bigger house. Is there any chance you can stock one of those? (Probably. Nothing is off limits when it comes to property in Ireland.)

Help!

According to some parenting experts it's never too early to involve your kids in chores around the house. Here's what we know about these experts. They don't have kids and they come from the same stable as those experts who suggested we should incorporate condoms into foreplay. (Because condoms are just so damn sexy.)

Anyway, here is what happens if you ask your kids to play some role in the great clear out. Nothing. Kids are incredibly sentimental, which is weird, because most of them don't drink wine. You'll struggle to throw away that €5.99 train set that nearly took Jack's hand off. 'But it's got my blood on it,' says Jack, weeping his little nostalgic tears. The two things you need to do for the great January Tidy-Up? Send the kids to their aunt's house and hire a skip.

3.4 RAIN PAIN

The definition of a dry day in Ireland is when it only rains for a small bit in the morning. If you think this doesn't matter when you have kids, wait until you try to put a toddler to bed when he's been confined indoors by the weather. It's like a double whammy.

I'm writing this in late May, with the weather forecast people promising some sun on our backs. There is a glow around when you can let the kids run wild in the evening after dinner. But this is payback time for those rainy days in late January when the sun couldn't be arsed rising, let alone shining down on you for a few days. Here's how one of those rainy winter days can pan out.

7.30 a.m. You awake to the sound of an angry mob flinging stones at your window. Hang on, it's just rain. Again. You check the hour-by-hour weather on your phone. There is only a 70% chance of rain between 10 a.m. and noon. You like those odds. Because you'll do anything to avoid yet another day of watching the *Twirlywoos* on a loop.

9.07 a.m. You're watching the *Twirlywoos* on a loop. It was either that or *Finding Nemo* and your two-year-old woke up with a fear of fish. You check the weather app on your phone. That 70% chance of rain icon has been replaced by a graphic showing a large monster shaking Ireland by the throat. This doesn't look good.

9.37 a.m. Your wife comes back from the gym, seven minutes late. You have an argument over who is taking more time away from the kids for their new exercise regime. That's what couples do in early January. You'll be back watching box sets on the couch together next week. So try not to make a big deal out of it.

12.30 p.m. You ask your four-year-old if she would like to go and see *The Good Dinosaur* at the local cinema in an hour's time. She says yes. Excellent. You will get three hours out of the house that involves a giant tub of rum and raisin ice cream. Your wife gets stuck at home with a two-year-old who is afraid of fish. Now that's what I call parenting.

1.55 p.m. You are kicked out of the cinema because your little girl can't stop crying. Apparently, you should have explained beforehand that instead of going to see an actual dinosaur, you were going to a 'stinky cold room with a big telly.' She cries all the way home. So do you, having calculated that the cost of a cinema trip for two means there is no summer holiday abroad this year. That means a fortnight in Ireland. Hence the tears.

2.30 p.m. You arrive home to find your wife working her way through a packet of Pringles and watching *Casablanca* on TV. The two-year-old, who never sleeps, has picked today for a two-hour nap. You make a mental note to get him back for this when he is old enough to understand the concept of revenge. The wife is two–nil up on you at this stage, given she already had a trip to the gym. You'll be doing well to salvage a draw.

3 p.m. You switch on the weather forecast on RTÉ. The forecaster is wearing a long black dress and black veil over her face. That's not a good sign.

3.15 p.m. Guilt. Lots of it. Your kids have been looking at one form of screen or another for six days in a row. You take out a jigsaw. Awww. What could be better than a family playing together on a rainy Saturday afternoon? Pretty much anything. The two-year-old actually manages to eat a piece of the jigsaw when no one is looking. We won't repeat what your four-year-old says when she discovers that the jigsaw can't be finished.

Let's just say she was listening to every word you shouted when United conceded a late equaliser last weekend. And you'd had two bottles of pale ale.

4 p.m. You take another look at the weather app on your phone because by now it is giving you a weird, cheap thrill. There is a yellow disc where the dark angry cloud should be. You look out the window and discover that the sun is shining. The Internet. It knows everything. You and your wife shift into 'get the kids out of the house for ten minutes of fresh air' mode.

4.20 p.m. Nothing to report. You are still trying to get the kids out of the house for ten minutes of fresh air.

4.40 p.m. Still nothing. The four-year-old is missing a glove.

5 p.m. You arrive at the local playground. It's dark and full of other families who haven't been out in a week. There is a clear divide in the playground. On one side you have parents who bought waterproof dungarees when they came into Lidl a few months ago. On the other are couples who are this close to getting a divorce. (You try to tell a toddler he can't go on a slide because it's wet.)

Parents who bought the dungarees are registering nine on the 'I'm So Smug Scale'. (That's where zero is 'not smug' and ten is Simon Cowell.) The good news is that you are one of those smug parents. All because your wife went down and queued up for a couple of pairs when they hit the shelves. That's almost enough for you to forgive her for being seven minutes late back from the gym. Almost.

And that's actually one of the good days. Here is a list of the things we have tried, with varying success, to keep little and big minds occupied through the wet days.

Painting

The average memory span of a parent with young kids? It's the period between the last time you tried to do painting with your kids and the moment you decide to do it again. Because you've obviously forgotten the two bottles of Pinot Grigio it took to calm down after the last attempt. Not to mention the cost of the contract cleaners.

Here's how it pans out. You spend thirty minutes preparing everything on the kitchen table, giving yourself all kinds of brownie points for not turning on the TV. Your children paint themselves for two minutes. They paint each other for four minutes. They start crying and say what they really want is a fort.

A Fort

Here's what you need for a fort. Two straight-backed chairs, one sheet and a large packet of chocolate biscuits. Leave out the biscuits if you believe those ads where kids stay in the one place for more than thirty seconds.

The trick is to wait at the entrance to the fort and hand over a biscuit every time one of them sticks her head out and says, 'Can we go swimming?' Make sure to have your phone ready so you can take thirty-seven photos and put up an incredibly smug Facebook post. (As if there's any other kind.) #FabForting #MagicMemories #IncredibleDad #LowSugar Biscuits #LookatMe.

The Museum

Here's a great one to ram down the throats of your friends

who bring their kids to Monkey Maze or Kidspace, when they should be filling their cute little heads with culture (for free).

That's the upside. There are a few downsides. You'd be surprised how little interest a child has in a 5,000-year-old chalice that was dug out of a bog. ('It's 5,000 years old, Jack.' 'I'm two and a half. And there's poo in my socks.') Worse again, it's a well-known fact that children run faster when they are around delicate, priceless artefacts, precariously balanced above a marble floor. Or, put another way, Jesus, me nerves.

Every time the kids think about the Bronze Age, they'll be reminded of you cursing at them in the National Museum. #MagicMemories #NotReally.

Movie Afternoon

You know why they call it movie afternoon? Because it's the kind of thing that only happens in a movie. Or in Californian families, which is the same thing. The notion that you and the kids can snuggle under a duvet and watch *Toy Story* on a wet and windy afternoon doesn't really work. Mainly because it's too long. *Toy Story* runs for eighty-one minutes. That's sixty-one minutes longer than your toddler can go without thinking, 'I'm going to get up and start running around in a circle for no reason.'

Worse again, they'll start doing this just as you start getting into the movie. Don't try to fight this. You'll just end up shouting, 'Can I not even get half an hour to watch a vaguely homoerotic story about a wooden cowboy and toy astronaut?' That's the kind of thing they'll repeat at playschool. #Morto.

Go Outside

We've all seen the weird family with two small kids out walking in the rain. There was a time when you'd laugh at them. Now you have kids of your own, they make you feel guilty. (Everything makes you feel guilty when you have kids of your own.)

That's why you end up buying all-weather gear for everyone that comes with something called a hurricane guarantee. You wait for a wet and windy day, then head out into the fray. After seven minutes your eldest child asks for a loan of your phone. You ask why. She says, 'I want to report you to the ISPCC.' You agree she has a point. On the way home, you pass the weird family walking in the rain. You wonder are they paid to do this by large corporations who make all-weather gear with hurricane guarantees. #TheySoAre.

The Shopping Centre

This is my favourite thing to do. Most shopping centres have a play area, with lots of soft surfaces for insurance reasons. The kids run around without hurting themselves (too much). You can take turns watching them, while the other half goes off and has a lie down in a changing room for thirty minutes. Plus the kids are tired enough to go to sleep later that night, after all the running around.

Just be careful how much you spend. Here's the typical bill for a trip to the shopping centre:

Toy bus ride where other parents wait for you to put in the money, before pushing their kids in too, €2.

Trip to McDonald's, €12.

Four shirts you buy in Zara because you haven't got the time to try them on, €100.

Flat White that you won't drink because that would involve relaxing for three minutes, €4.

Another trip to McDonald's because you know the way you're starving again after thirty minutes, €12.

Another toy bus ride because it is impossible to get to the car park without passing at least three of them, €2.

So, while it's a great way to spend a rainy day, make sure to do your sums. Because it might actually be cheaper to build your own shopping centre out the back.

Wash the Duckies

What's Wash the Duckies? This is where you put a safe amount of water in the sink and invite your two-year-old to wash his plastic ducks. (With any luck, he might wash himself by accident and spare you the bother of giving him a shower later on.)

All being well you'll get a good hour's peace, freeing you up to do important work like spying on your cousin on Facebook. You'll know when this hour is up because there will be water flowing down the stairs. #Sendmoretowels

Baking

The pleasure you get from baking with kids is inversely proportional to the number of children you have. Baking with one child is one of life's great delights. Doing it with two or more children can use up what's left of your nerves. Mainly because you have only one pair of eyes and you never really get margarine out of a child's hair. (Unless of course you wash it. But who has time for that?)

3.5 IS IT REALLY A HOLIDAY?

I'll never forget the misery of Lanzarote. Freda, our eldest, was just over six months old. We reckoned we had earned a break, so we booked a week in late February. I'd like to meet the person who came up with the notion that you are guaranteed winter sunshine in the Canaries. It was 16 degrees and windy.

The weather was only a small part of the problem though. What really struck us was that holidays as we knew them were over. Eating what we liked when we liked, drinking at lunchtime, napping in the afternoon, dinner at 10 p.m., actually wanting to have sex – all that was gone.

You see, no one told Freda she was in Lanzarote. She still wanted to sleep and eat at her usual times. It didn't matter to her that there was a great little Italian place at the bottom of the hill. (There wasn't by the way, there wasn't a great little anything, anywhere. But we'll leave eating in Lanzarote for another book.) The net result of flying 2,500 kilometres was that she found it harder to go to sleep in a strange cot.

Six months later we brought her for a short break to the north of Spain. (This was when we still thought we had money.) The sun shone, Freda paddled in the sea, we had two *pains au chocolat* each with our breakfast. It wasn't our old, pre-child holidays, but it was magic in comparison to Lanzarote.

Our holidays with the kids keep getting better as they get older. They're five and three now, we're just back from the south of France and it was the best holiday we ever had. (The campsite south of France, as opposed to the 'Ooh, look, it's another Russian oligarch' south of France, before you ask.)

That's why I put the holiday section here, rather than earlier in the book. Because taking a small child abroad can end up as a harsh and expensive lesson. My advice is to wait until they are at least well past one before shepherding them through an airport, but if you can do without guaranteed sunshine, wait another year until they are two.

Here are the major things you need to consider, before you head away.

Bring Your Mother-in-Law

Seriously, do. As I said above, there is a shock waiting for anyone who goes on holiday for the first time with a small child. The shock is that it isn't a holiday. Unless you enjoy trying to purée sweet potato with a fork because the apartment doesn't have a blender. Or you are Victoria Beckham. (In which case 'Hi, Your Beckhamness, any chance we could have a loan of one of your nannies for the first fortnight in July? Seriously, you'll hardly miss her.')

There are a couple of golden rules for first-timers. The first is if your child doesn't eat in a restaurant in Ireland, they won't eat in one abroad. That's a shame, because it's so much cheaper. The second rule is your partner will resent having to string out a glass of red wine all evening if she is breastfeeding. Particularly since you have a pint in each hand in an attempt to get loaded before the baby starts bawling and you have to retreat back to the apartment. There are a couple of ways to describe this scene. Romantic isn't one of them. Particularly since there are two hours of cleaning to be done in said apartment when you get back. (Don't ask me why, there just is.)

The only solution is to bring some help in the form of your in-laws. Who knew they could come in so handy?

Staycation 3: This Time it's Pouring

There is a telling bit of dialogue at the end of a particularly crazy episode of *Father Ted*:

Ted: 'So, have you learned anything from your experience?'
Dougal: 'No.'

We're all a bit Dougal when it comes to going on holidays in Ireland. Years of experience tell us that the Irish summer starts with a shower in late May that lasts until the first week of September. Bizarrely, it only takes one semi-decent summer for us to forget this undeniable truth. A week of sunshine in June and the Dougal inside our head is already on DoneDeal, trying to get a good price for a house in Dunmore East during August.

Once booked, our Dougal head will spend every waking hour in the next six weeks looking at weather websites with names like WeAreMakingThisUp.ie. The hope, the hope, it will drive you crazy in the end. Unless spending ten days trapped in a small house in Waterford with your kids gets there first. Which it will. Stay in Ireland if you must, but I reckon nothing beats the promise of a few days' sun on your back. It's often enough to keep me going through the winter.

Flight Costs

There are three ways to get a cheap flight. The first is to wait for Aer Lingus or Ryanair to have a one-day flash sale. These are great if you want to fly to Düsseldorf on a Monday night in late April. (No two-year-old ever went to bed and had a dream about Düsseldorf.)

The second is to check the airline websites four times a day to see if that flight to Barcelona has come down. The main problem there is a sense that the airline is tracking your every move and knows you are desperate. Sometimes it can feel like Michael O'Leary is lurking outside your house, listening in on your conversations. (We can't rule that out. Maybe use hand-signals when discussing holiday plans with your partner, just to be on the safe side.)

The third way to fly on the cheap is to use a flight booking site like Skyscanner, KAYAK or Google Flights. They are good at unearthing cut-price flights, if you are willing to go through the UK. The danger there is you might book one of them. Because nothing says 'I'm on holidays' less than nine hours in Luton Airport with three kids under seven. Don't even think about it.

Of course, a lot of people take long flights with toddlers under two, when they can still fly for free. I recommend you go to New York, Los Angeles, Buenos Aires and then Sydney. I also recommend you leave your toddler at home.

Seriously, it will cost you the same and you'll have a much better time. Unless you think the one thing missing when you wake hungover and jet-lagged in LA is a little person trying to vomit on your head.

Where in the World?

Two weeks in a French campsite is always a good bet. Just make sure there is no major sporting event in the vicinity, because the fans love a campsite. There is every chance the mobile home next to yours will be host to three guys from Burnley. Very nice lads, but there is no upside to someone singing 'You Fat Bastard' at three in the morning. Particularly if your partner has just given birth and feels a bit touchy about her weight.

The eastern Med is pretty much off limits because of the threat of terrorism. The States can be expensive with a strong dollar, and anyway Donald Trump won't let you in. So now is the time to start looking for flights to Spain, France or Italy.

There is something you should know about Spain. It's full of Spaniards. Or more to the point, it's full of Spanish kids. I reckon every last one of them is actually a model. Which means your Sophie could end up looking like a foxy spud-head next to a gang of them down by the pool.

There is no point in trying to compete by decking her head to toe in clothes from Zara. Ten minutes after you get off the plane, it's clear the Spaniards have a network of exclusive Zaras just for themselves. Stand one of them next to Prince George and you'd swear his Royalness got his clothes in a lucky bag. That's the level you're playing at in Spain.

It gets worse. The gorgeous little models are also incredibly well behaved. It's all *por favor* and *gracias Mama* with that lot. Meanwhile your Jack is trying to set fire to Barcelona. It's hard to know what to do here. Maybe try Portugal. I hear their kids are out of control as well.

City Breaker?

You really want to be one of those couples? You know, the ones who don't let a small child affect how they live their lives. The same ones who go on a statement city break with said small child to show that some things will never change. Here's some advice. Take a trip to San Sebastian or Valencia before you have a baby.

See that couple with a buggy, in the buzzy tapas bar? Just there in the corner – you can't miss them. She's face down in a bowl of squid trying to get a bit of kip. You would be too, if thirty Spanish teenagers decided to stop for a chat outside your city-centre apartment at 5.30 a.m. Spanish teenagers are very, very excitable people at 5.30 a.m. Or, as it's known locally, Scooter Time. That's when Spanish people all start their scooters at the same time and drive around in circles for an hour. Look, back in the tapas bar, now the father has gone face first into his patatas bravas. They are all asleep. Except, of course, for the child in the buggy. The child never sleeps on a city break.

In case you haven't guessed, I reckon your city break days are over for a few years. It can be hard to know what a small kid is thinking. But I'm fairly certain it isn't, 'I'd love to stay up until 2 a.m., wolfing down calamari and small beers.'

Apartment or Mobile Home?

It's ridiculous to say you can't swing a cat in a mobile home. The truth is you can't swing a cat anywhere. They just won't let you.

Still, for all the turning sideways involved in getting into the jacks, the mobile home has a lot going for it. The best being that you can sit out on the deck and judge your neighbours for poisoning their kids. (That couple from Kildare are feeding their kids pizza again, Joe. We're so much better than them.)

The paper-thin walls are also a huge advantage. Nothing beats the sound of someone else's kids crying. It could be you. But it isn't. Sweet. The only drawback is when you end up next to a German couple who have the best sex life in Europe and don't mind who knows about it. All that 'Oh, mein Gott, ja' at two in the morning can make you feel bad about your twice a month. (Maybe twice a week on holidays, cheap wine is good that way.)

To Package or Not to Package?

You know the way you would like to organise the holiday from scratch, rather than book a package, because you are a wizard on the Internet and incredibly good at squirrelling out cheap deals. Well, consider this scenario. Your flight into Barcelona-Reus is delayed for two hours. There is nobody at the Los Dodgissimo Motors desk. That's because there isn't a Los Dodgissimo Motors desk. Someone points towards a plastic cabin out in the dark distance beyond the entrance to the airport. You head off, pushing two trolleys of luggage while herself pushes a screaming toddler in the buggy. Just as you arrive at the closed and unattended cabin for Los Dodgissimo Motors, a coach passes by, carrying people from your flight who booked a package holiday.

Here's the question. Will your partner A: say nothing, because that would only make things worse? Or B: point out that she wanted to book a package holiday in a sentence that includes the words useless and gobshite? If you answered B, you know what to do. Book a package holiday.

If the answer is A, then you still need to get the transport bit right. Here's a sentence you'll never hear from Irish Dad. 'Let's just get a taxi from the airport, I have no problem with being driven around by another man.' You see, Irish Dad isn't allowed to make many important decisions in life. But he still retains the right to get lost in a foreign country. And so do you. That's why you might insist on hiring a car to make the ten-minute drive from the airport to an all-in resort which you never have to leave. That's actually a three-hour drive once you get your hands on it. Only a fool would use the satnav on their phone in a foreign country, says you, missing the turn off the motorway for the third time.

Here's my experience. Queuing with kids for a hire car when you are just off a flight is like going for a bath with a shark. The potential downside is huge. Particularly if you went for the cheapest car-hire firm, even though 87,000 people went on to TripAdvisor to say the guy behind the desk at the airport was called Fat Tony and the whole thing was a cover for the local mafia.

So go with an international outfit whose name you recognise. You'll find reviews for their operation at your destination airport on TripAdvisor and rentalcars.com. (Ignore the ten worst reviews, the world is full of cranks.) And finally, if you are the kind of person who tends to get lost in Ireland, you will probably get lost abroad. In which case, I'd recommend you look up the price of airport transfers or taxis. Because nerves are usually running on empty for a few hours after you arrive.

If you really have to drive, Google Maps will allow you to download a map to your phone, so you don't have to worry about racking up a massive data bill trying to find your campsite. Put that on your list of things to do before taking off.

And Finally … How's Your Dad Bod?

It isn't just women who put on weight after having a child. (I wouldn't share this insight with herself; just picture where that conversation will go and you'll see why.) A new kid around the house means a lot of chocolate rewards and limited time for exercise. This is fine in Ireland, where you can hide the results under seven jumpers. But that can be quite uncomfortable when it's 27 degrees. And so is flashing your man boobs at a group of tanned, unsuspecting Dutch types around the pool. Worse again, a lot of French campsites insist that men wear Speedos. This seems like a deliberate attempt to embarrass Irish men.

You can do what you want with this information. I'd recommend you put down the chocolate in late April and start picking up the bell bars. You don't want to look bad next to the Dutch.

By the way, here is something that could happen to your partner. I've heard it described as 'The Cambrils Park Experience'. (Cambrils Park is a campsite south of Barcelona very popular with Irish parents.) The experience could be described as 'Walking Around In My Knickers in Front of People I Vaguely Know from College'. Here is how it happens. Your wife or partner keeps bumping into people she knew from college and school around the resort. It's fine at first, until she starts to suspect that one or two of the lads are having a perv. From then on she says she feels like she is walking around in her knickers. Try not to laugh when she tells you about this. That's just not supportive.

Okay, now that all the planning is done, it's actually time to go on holidays. Here are my dos and don'ts:

> **Don't go near the packing.** Your partner will want to bring winter clothes even though you are going to Spain and it's July. There is nothing you can do to stop her; THERE IS NOTHING SHE CAN DO TO STOP HER! So butt out. You don't want to have any responsibility for the packing. Unless you want to spend seven days in Mallorca repeating the phrase 'I didn't think we'd need it.' In fairness, you weren't to know you'd need to bring an ironing board on holiday.
>
> Look, going on holidays with kids is basically a challenge for your wife, to see if she can fit your whole house into three suitcases. The best thing you can do is take the kids away for a few hours while she gives that a go. It's best they don't hear the cursing that goes on when herself is in Packing Mode. Just don't be surprised when you get back and she says, 'Nearly there, I never knew it would be so difficult to get the hedge trimmer into our cabin luggage.'
>
> And, by the way, keep your views to yourself when she insists on checking in a separate bag for her shoes. Women like to bring all their shoes on holidays. There's nothing anyone can do about it.

Don't fall for a nice cup of tea. It is deeply ingrained in the Irish psyche to never say no to a cup of tea. It has served us well down the ages, in all kinds of situations. One exception is when you are strapped in a seat at 33,000 feet. And not just because the tea costs more than the flight. It turns out there is actually one thing more nerveracking than getting through airport security with kids. And that's putting a cup of steaming hot water between two wriggling toddlers. So say no to tea.

Don't hop on a bus. Any money saved here will be pumped into relationship counselling when you get home. If you want to see why, you can simulate the experience before you head away. Just buy a blowtorch and keep your child awake all night. The next morning, walk to a nearby bus-stop with said child, heating both of you with the blowtorch while your wife insists you should have turned right at the top of the hill. That's what it's like getting a bus in southern Europe in summertime with a child in tow. If you're lucky.

Don't fall into the octopus trap. You can't get bacon and cabbage in Portugal. That's a good enough reason to go there. But it means you're down one of your mash 'em up farmer's dinners with spuds. You might feel a temptation to put an octopus salad in front of your child, mainly so you can post a photo on Facebook with the hashtag, #AmazingParentOrWhat?' You should resist this temptation with the same vigour that your child will resist anything that looks like it came from the sea. Just buy the nuggets and move on. Or get some grilled fish and ketchup and see how you go. (This actually worked for us in France. Amazing parents or what? Even if it was all about the ketchup.)

Don't bother with culture. It's probably intellectual insecurity, but a certain type of person feels they need to take in 'a bit of culture' when they travel abroad. You will see them dragging their kids to a local cathedral, which is funny, because they deliberately sent them to an Educate Together and wouldn't go near a church at home.

There is also an easy way to spot these families at the departure gate on the way home. They're the ones with the morbidly obese kids, after all the ice-cream bribes. So take a holiday from all this and don't bother with the bit of culture you sampled before the kids. Which, let's face it, mainly involved ducking into an art gallery to get out of the heat.

Don't avoid the Irish. We all know, deep down, that it's impossible to avoid Irish people on holidays. Take a trip around the scorching, tiny streets in some closed city in Yemen; you are still guaranteed to bump into a guy called Ciaran wondering if you know the score in the Tipperary match.

Still, you'll find the 'bit of culture' person mentioned above will always go out of his way to avoid Irish people on holidays. This is fine when you don't have kids, because that guy in the Celtic jersey from Kildare would wear you down in the end. But picking a strip of coast that's popular with the Dutch won't cut it when you have kids. And not just because a Dutch toddler has better English than yourself. (Well, better English than the guy from Kildare anyway.) Or that next to the tanned Dutch kids, your little spud-heads look like Wayne Rooney on a bad hair day.

The real problem with this strip of coast is that the kids' clubs are run in Dutch. That means your kids will be with you all day. Think about that for a while. And maybe book a holiday in Torremolinos.

Don't forget the iPad. Forget about a room with a view. What you need is a device to play that memory stick of movies your cousin got from a guy at work called Dodgy Donie. (Again, you downloaded them yourself, but no one admits that in public.) Trust me, when it's 32 degrees outside there is only one female that can bring back some pre-kids magic to your holiday in the sun. And her name is Peppa Pig.

Four Things You Must Do:

1: Seven euro minimum on wine

It's as easy to get a bottle of wine for €3.50 on holidays as it is to get a hangover to last until mid-afternoon. The fact that it's called Vin du Paddy Pisshead should have given you a clue. Spend a bit extra. Every euro is another hour off your hangover.

2: Check in at least one bag

Even if it costs more than the flight. (Or your car, judging by charges for a bag these days.) Otherwise, you'll become that couple trying to get liquids out of their carry-on luggage at security, while managing two kids. They're divorced now, you know.

3: Ban the phone

No mobile phone use after 7 p.m. every evening. Talk to your partner over a glass of wine instead. I know it's scary, but it needs to be done. Who knows where it might lead?

4: Forget about it

That thing that's been bothering you? Forget about it for a week or two. You're messing around in the sun with your kids. It actually doesn't get much better than this.

3.6 EMBRACE THE TELLY

Why does Homer Simpson hug his television regularly? Because he has three kids. Before your lot arrive, you might plan to ration their TV consumption, so they will have more time for reading and colouring-books. Good luck with that. You'll end up reading a story about a, frankly, weird relationship between a giraffe and a caterpillar, fourteen times in a row. And kids don't colour in books; they colour in walls. So, face up to the fact that the telly is a vital part of your child-rearing toolbox.

The single best thing I bought when our first child arrived was a Chromecast device for our TV. At one level, Chromecast is a yoke you plug into a spare HDMI port that allows you to play YouTube videos and more on your TV. At another, more important level, it has stopped us from going bonkers. Why? Well, give a toddler your phone so she can watch *Peppa Pig* and I guarantee she will sign you up for Tinder. And no one will believe that's what happened.

I play the kids a YouTube video on TV at least once a day. Usually when I want them to leave me alone in the kitchen so I can eat a minimum of three chocolate biscuits. It's the kind of time out we can all appreciate. We have also developed a habit of playing old Silly Symphony cartoons when they are getting ready for bed. A particular favourite is *Lullaby Land*. If you think this a sweet little cartoon with a nice song, then you have no idea what cartoon makers were thinking in 1933. It's a kind of waking nightmare, where dancing safety-pins, lit matches and boogie men chase a child along in his dreams. Our kids love it to bits and it doesn't affect their sleep.

They love all the old-school cartoons, made before a more sensitive type of world decided that it wasn't okay to shove a coyote off a cliff. Our kids howl with laughter at *Road Runner*, *Tom and Jerry* and *Bugs Bunny*. The more outrageous the better, and we get to relive some magic cartoon moments from our youth. Here's hoping it doesn't turn the kids into sadistic chainsaw murderers.

Here are some other shows on YouTube that can help rear your kids.

Baby Mozart

Baby Mozart is a twenty-six-minute video that is guaranteed to hypnotise a young baby. In fact, it's still a favourite for our five-year-old. The video is junior eye-candy, with colourful toys in motion set to a soundtrack of Mozart music. It's ideal if you are looking to hypnotise a child on a long flight. (I can't imagine why you wouldn't want to do that.)

The beauty of *Baby Mozart* is people will admire you for

giving your child a bit of culture at a young age. What they don't realise is the song might as well be *Agadoo* – the baby is just mesmerised by a toy bear playing the drums.

Peppa Pig

The only show that works for adults and toddlers. Used correctly, this show will keep a lid on your kids during the tricky eighteen months to three years of age stretch. A note of caution – there are three problems with Peppa. The first is accent. Peppa and family are a posh bunch, so there is every chance your little one will end up sounding like Binky from *Made in Chelsea*. You mightn't have a problem with this if you come from a county where the local accent is considered a liability. (Hello Monaghan!)

The second, related issue is the Pigs live a very posh lifestyle. So you might have to face some awkward questions as to why you are not going skiing during mid-term. Unless of course you are going skiing during mid-term, in which case, look at you all loaded and any chance of a loan?

The third problem is you will spend the price of your child's education on merchandise like Peppa wellies, just to get your daughter to stop nagging you. Trust me, that's still a price worth paying.

Ben and Holly

No, your ears aren't deceiving you. A lot of people who do the voices on *Peppa Pig* also crop up on this show, aimed at slightly older kids. It's like the producers plan to capture a lifelong audience with a bunch of familiar characters in different shows. In twenty years' time your kids will be watching a Scandinavian crime noir series, where Pedro Pony will be chasing the killer of Suzy Sheep.

Instead of the mildly hilarious middle-class family life in *Peppa Pig*, *Ben and Holly* is set in a magical kingdom full of smug elves. It's not as bad as it sounds. (It couldn't be, says you.) The jokes are good and the message is more British than American. This matters, because there is only so much American positivity you can take after a week without sleep. (Try none.)

Mr Bloom's Nursery

This is based in a nursery garden where all the vegetables are played by puppets. The kids would love to get their hands on one of those puppets. A lot of moms would love to get their hands on the gardener, Mr Bloom. Apparently, the cute actor who plays the gardener gets red-hot fan mail from some moms, with saucy comments about popular root crops that have no place in a family book like this one.

I don't mind Mr Bloom. He is unusual among children's television presenters, in that he seems like a normal human being. Or at least someone who you would let within 100 metres of your kids. Most other presenters have a kind of nailed-on crazy smile to hide their disappointment that they are still jumping around, pretending to be three.

So, there's something for everyone in *Mr Bloom's Nursery*. Except Dad, who gets to sit there while Mom says things like, 'Ooh, I wouldn't mind having a look at his radishes.' The things we have to put up with.

Kipper the Dog

It's like *Seinfeld* for toddlers, mixed with a little bit of *Last of the Summer Wine*. Nothing much ever happens to Kipper and his friends. Anything that does happen, happens at a very slow pace. This is the show to stick on in the evening to wind everybody down a few notches before you summon up the energy to put them to bed.

(You'll need energy to put them to bed, by the way. The main reason children go to bed late is because their parents can't find enough energy to get up off the couch and start looking for pyjamas.)

Franklin or Paw Patrol?

Try neither. *Franklin* is a Canadian cartoon about an incredibly nerdy turtle. He is so good and obedient you feel like offering him a cigarette. A cheerful conformist might go down well in Canada, but they're generally not liked over here. So I'd recommend you don't let your kids watch *Franklin*. He'll just be a bad influence.

The same goes for the do-gooders on *Paw Patrol*. It's a horribly nice show about dogs who rescue people, the exact opposite of the fun available from *Road Runner*, or the gentle cynicism of *Ben and Holly*.

That said, my kids go mad for *Paw Patrol*. And in the end, if they love it, I love it. Because the minute a child loses interest in a video, they come looking for you. That usually means stuffing a chocolate biscuit into your pocket because if they see it, they'll want it, and bad things happen when kids eat chocolate after 6 p.m.

The take-away here is it's possible to both love and hate a show, as long as it takes up 100% of my kids' attention.

3.7 TIME FOR SCHOOL

If you haven't put your child's name down for fourteen schools by now, you need to get a move on. You'll learn a lot a lot about yourself during the school choosing process. Are you a snob? How much of a snob? What do you really think of the Catholic Church? Do you think the school you went to determined what you did in life? Does it matter that the school allows you to take your kids out in early June so you can get a cheaper summer holiday? Are you selfish enough to factor traffic volumes into your choice?

We went all around the houses trying to pick the right place. We met principals, checked feeder options for secondary schools, spoke to teachers we knew, wondered if the place would be more about crowd control than education. In the end we chose the school around the corner. It isn't in the poshest part of town, but then neither are we.

It actually makes a lot of sense to pick a school where our kids will be around kids like them. Freda was accepted into a school in a more well-heeled area, but we could see the downside of her being in a class where the kids' parents were better off than us. We didn't want to be the ones telling her she couldn't join her pals on a school skiing trip. And we reckon sending her local will stand to her in later life, rather than holding her back.

Here's a run-through of the decisions you need to make.

How Soon is Too Soon?

When should you put your child's name down for a school? To answer this, you need to understand Cambrils Envy. This is the feeling parents get during January every year when they try to book Cambrils camping park near Barcelona and discover it is booked out. We've all been there.

Likewise, we've all had to listen to friends who booked it the previous October because they didn't want to miss out. These people are everywhere. They also put their kids down for schools before they are even born, usually when Mom starts to ovulate. The point is, it's never too soon. If you haven't had a child yet, but are going out on a promising date tomorrow with a girl who might be the one, here is my advice: start ringing around some schools. And wear your blue shirt on the date, that colour really suits you.

Bear in mind, like us, you'll probably end up with your child's name on the list for every school in a ten-kilometre radius. It wasn't until we sent our kids to pre-school and got a flavour of how education might work that we were in a position to make a well-informed decision. So there's no huge rush. But it helps to keep as many options open as possible.

As Gaeilge?

The school around the corner that we chose is also a Gaelscoil. This is odd, because I always thought I was about as likely to join the IRA as I was to send my kids to a school run through Irish. I can still remember the crippling despair I felt heading into a double-Irish class when I was at school myself. But we sent our eldest to the pre-school (*naíonra*) for the Gaelscoil, to see if it was an option. Now that Irish is a language that Freda speaks a little, when she comes home every day I love the sound of every word out of her mouth. Okay, it needs a bit more work on our part to make sure we can help with the homework. But I can see it working for us and her, over time. There is every chance you'll think differently.

Losing your Religion?

A word of warning on Educate Together schools. The parents are expected to take a very active role in fund-raising and running the school. This is obviously a disaster for anyone who is hoping to drop their kids off to school in the morning and pick them up when they are eighteen. (Hello you!) That's why a lot of Catholic parents still send their kids to a Catholic school. I'd like to say you shouldn't feel guilty about this. But telling a Catholic to stop feeling guilty is like telling a crocodile to stop eating fish.

Some people send their kids to a Catholic school but don't enrol them for communion. (We're doing that.) Here's the rule of thumb. A seven-year-old boy won't notice that other boys in his class are preparing for communion, as long as you buy him a bike. However, tell a seven-year-old girl she is not allowed to wear a wedding dress and act like a princess for a day, and she will join the nuns just to spite you.

Apparently, parents are making it up to kids who didn't get to make communion by bringing them on a treat-break for a couple of days. Seriously, I'm not making that up. So you might want to price in a trip to Disneyland Paris to make up for the fact that you wouldn't let your daughter 'get married'.

I'm not making that up either. That's what my daughter calls it.

Whatever you choose, it's important to never lose the real meaning of First Holy Communion. A chance to lash on *My Big Gypsy Wedding* levels of false tan and drink Prosecco in the afternoon. No wonder it remains so popular.

Other Parents

Obviously, you're not a snob. But that won't stop you driving by a school at 3 p.m. to do the Sportswear Test on the waiting parents. Gym gear on a slim lady means the school is popular with nice, responsible parents like yourself. A tracksuit on a pudgy man means the exact opposite, and there goes that school off the possibles list.

However, you'll need to come up with a different reason for taking that school off the list, because as we know, you're not a snob. A great one is to tell your friends that the traffic around school-drop time is awful. The beauty of this is that it is always true. That's because of the parents driving by at 5 kilometres per hour to perform the Sportswear Test. They're a bloody menace.

Traffic

You should know that school selection means different things to moms and dads. Mom is mainly interested in student–teacher ratios, extra-curricular activities and feeder potential for secondary schools. Dad is more interested in how he might drive there. He put the school into his satnav and it came back with a route which is fine for someone who lacks Dad's incredible knowledge of traffic dynamics in the local area.

In fairness, Google Maps wasn't to know that the milk delivery van is often parked outside the Centra at 8.13 a.m., which can cause mayhem for miles around. Dad has discussed this with his best friend Larry, who was quick to praise Dad for his excellent insight. Both Dad and Larry agree that it would be crazy to send the child to that school. Unless the milk delivery guy changes schedule and then it's everyone back to the drawing board.

3.8 CAN'T STAND THE HEAT? GET INTO THE KITCHEN.

It was an Italian who taught me how to cook. It was when I shared an apartment in Germany with a guy from Padova, who was pretty good at attracting women with food. I'd arrive in to find yet another blonde sitting at our dinner table as Marco did his thing with an aubergine. (Enough of the giggles.) It became clear I should learn how to cook.

This was the mid-1990s, when most Irish guys wouldn't have known what to do with an egg. So when I got back to Ireland and knew how to cook pasta *al dente,* people thought I was some kind of Jamie Oliver, without the cute wife.

Not for long. I landed a cute wife of my own a few years later, after cooking her some chicken parm. I continued doing the cooking before the kids came along. I was working from home and I like cooking, so it made sense that I made dinner. Then, when our daughter Freda came along, my wife was on maternity leave and slowly edged me out of the kitchen. She's a better cook than me now, not least because she has a sense for what the kids will eat. (That's actually the definition of a good cook when you have kids.)

I'm learning from her now and have found my way back to the cooker. It's still a great way to relax and free up your mind for a while, particularly when they start to eat the same food as yourself. It's not going to attract new women into my life, but who has time for that when you have two kids under five? (And a gorgeous wife you wouldn't swap for anything. Hi honey!)

Obviously, all kids are different, but here's the food we cook to guarantee that everyone gets to look forward to mealtime.

It Starts with Chicken

You can cook a roast chicken for dinner on Sunday, make curry with the leftovers on Monday, boil up the carcass and use the stock for soup, and your kids will love all of it to bits. That's the good news.

The bad news is that at some point they will look at the chicken, look at you, look back at the chicken and say, 'Why does it look like a birdy?' This is grand if you have twins or triplets, because they are all ready for the 'where meat comes from' chat at the same time. The problem arises when you tell your five-year-old the grisly truth and she tells her three-year-old brother, who then cries for a month. The only way to make him stop? Chicken nuggets. (No one said kids are consistent.)

Bacon Is Your Friend

Sorry, I don't mean rasher sandwiches. The days when you could live off those for a weekend are gone, unless you want your kids to feature in a TV series called *Their Parents Should be Ashamed of Themselves*. The bacon I'm talking about here is back bacon, the wobbly hunk of meat with a slice of fat on top. It's the kind of thing we serve to Yanks in hotels, covered in something called Killarney Sauce. Here's the truth about bacon. It's delicious, as long as you leave out the Killarney Sauce and get it from the butcher's. (Supermarket bacon can taste of air.)

Proper bacon flavours cabbage (or turnip*) when you cook them in the same pot. The kids love it mashed together with spuds and they'll eat it for two days on the trot. Like I say, bacon is your friend. Just don't tell any of your friends who don't have kids. They'll feel sorry for you.

* Slice the turnip very thinly and cook for three hours.

Fishy?

The definition of smug? A parent watching their child eating fish. It's perfectly acceptable to post a photo on Instagram with the caption: #I'mBetterThanYou. (Unless the fish in question is in finger form and came in a Happy Meal – that's the definition of over-reach.)

So, how do you get your child to eat fish? Ask a Spaniard. Spaniards aren't afraid of fish like we are. A friend of mine from Madrid showed me how it's done, when feeding her twins. Marinade flat fish (lemon sole or plaice) in olive oil, balsamic vinegar and chopped garlic for 30 minutes. Dip in flour, then beaten egg and place skin-side-down on a medium heated pan, with oil and a little butter. Three minutes either side, then serve it up with oven chips and a huge dollop of ketchup, just in case. There you go. #YouAreSoSmug.

Barbecue

If you haven't got a barbecue, get one. Not least because you can warn the kids to stay clear of the flames, freeing you up to enjoy an uninterrupted beer in the sun. What a result.

A lot of men are taking up smoking now, as in those low 'n' slow charcoal smokers where you stand watching a pork shoulder cooking for eight hours while your wife looks after the kids. If you are one of these men, then here is my proposition – let's swap wives. Because mine would never fall for that carry-on.

There's no real time for charcoal when there are small kids buzzing around your back yard. (It's not exactly safe, either.) Basically, you can't go wrong with a three-burner gas barbecue for about €250. Everything tastes better after being cooked outdoors. And steak, charred pepper and corn-on-the-cob is a welcome break from a long, dark winter of stews and spag bol.

Spag Bol

You'll often hear parents saying, 'We could always just give them spaghetti Bolognese.' It's like it's cheating because it's related to pizza. But it isn't. Particularly if you steam a sweet potato and mash it into the sauce. (If you don't hide a super-food in your child's dinner these days, someone will probably call social services.)

This guilt-free spag bol lies at the heart of your 'give them something quick and we'll have a takeaway when they are in bed' strategy. Remember to throw in some red wine for extra flavour, which officially allows you to down a glass as it cooks. Just try not to say, 'One glass for the kids and one for me', when you are pouring. It doesn't really sound great when you say it out loud.

Turning Japanese?

There is an amazing Japanese takeaway near us in Cork. I'm not telling you the name, because the queues are bad enough as it is. It's the kind of food we like after we've placated the kids with healthy spag bol. The best way to describe the food is that it gives you a hug. Which is why we decided to get it early one day and give it to the little one. Kids love hugs, right? Wrong. I'll never forget the face my daughter made, once she was finished spitting out every last one of the grains of rice. She actually stayed cross with us for hours. This is just a long way of saying that your kids mightn't like seaweed. So, be careful how you go.

Spud Heads

Spuds get a bad rap, because our mother gave us potatoes and what would she know? (Everything, but you can't admit it.) But here's the thing – our kids love potatoes. They love them mashed with gravy, mashed with cabbage or peas, roasted, they love steamed baby potatoes cut in half, or fried potatoes made with leftover spuds from dinner the day before. We haven't given them baked potatoes yet, but it is only a matter of time. As for chips, they are all over everything from an oven chip to the chunky fellas you get in the chipper.

It's almost like the kids understand that spuds are grown locally, are good for vitamin C, fibre and potassium, and they fill you up quickly. So, give your kids quinoa or wholewheat pasta or whatever, if it makes you feel better. But I'm not sure it will make your kids feel better. Because kids love spuds.

Dad's Standby

The only thing my father could cook was sausages. That's why we were always trying to get my mother to shag off on holiday by herself; we just loved sausages. (We loved you too Mum, but it's hard to compete with bangers.)

To honour this, I have a down and dirty Dad's Dinner. Fish fingers, fried eggs and beans, that's what they get when they come in from school every Friday. There are two upsides here. The first is I can see they love me a little bit more every week, particularly if I pile on the ketchup. The second positive is even more important. I get to eat it too. It's a genuine treat to have Truck-Stop nosh after five days of bacon, gravy, chicken, stew and cabbage. So pick out your favourite junk meal now and make sure your kids get a taste for it. Because there is no better way to generate a bit of Friday feeling.

3.9 DO YOU DIY?

Not if you are anything like me. I have big, awkward fingers and I'm hopeless with shapes. (I failed all the 2D and 3D aptitude tests in school.) That said, you never really grow up until you have kids. And growing up, when you're a man, means hanging a towel rail in the bathroom, even when you don't feel like it.

The stakes are a lot higher when you have kids. Back in your single days, it was actually funny when that press you hung in the jacks fell down a week later because you used the wrong Rawlplug. Now, it might fall on a child. So, you do need to up your game a bit.

I steered clear of DIY, initially, when the kids were very small, because it's not the type of thing you should take up after twenty-three sleepless nights. But, once they settled down to twelve hours a night, I had no excuse and it was time to take out some tools.

Here is the little bit I've learned on the DIY front. You can probably skip this section if you are handy around the house. (Before you go, is there any chance you could come around to my place this weekend? There's a leak in the shower.)

The Tools

The first tool you should get is an in-law who knows how to use a drill. (I'm not suggesting my brother-in-laws are 'tools'; they've pretty much built half my house.)

Having a person in the know means you have someone to call when your partner says you need to fix the ceiling. The fact that it's her brother you are calling could be seen as an embarrassment, so I tend to do a fair bit of texting on the sly.

Watching the in-laws has taught me the most important thing about DIY. And that is I'll never be any good at DIY. I lack the patience for it, I don't have the curiosity and I'm not great at anything that involves precision. That said, DIY prowess is seen as a virtue in my wife's family, which means I have had to learn some basic skills so they don't think I'm a dingbat. Thanks to my in-laws, I can hang a shelf without drilling through an electric wire. It's better than nothing.

A Guy for That

You can't keep relying on your in-laws. Particularly if they look for a favour in return and you end up spending a weekend painting their walls. (It's bad enough making a mess in your own place.) The key is to find a handyman who won't charge the earth. Your gut instinct here is to find an ugly guy so your wife won't fall in love with him. That's actually a mistake. The only way your partner will allow you to hire a guy is if said guy could pass for Bradley Cooper. 'Sounds like a job for Bradley,' says she, counting the minutes to his arrival. We call it win–win in our place. 'Bradley' loves it too.

The Basics

I actually have a toolbox. My in-laws call over sometimes so they can point at it and laugh. (I'm their DIY Clown as a form of payment for all the work they do.) This toolbox includes:

- A thirty-six-piece screwdriver head set, including Phillips, flat and Allen key. I only ever use one of the Phillips heads, but having the set makes it look like I'm ready for business.

- Two retractable tape measures, one for me and the other for the kids so I can distract them when I'm trying to measure a wall.

- A small hammer, so I can hit myself on the thumb a few times a year.

- A large spirit measure, for hanging cupboards on the bathroom wall. A small spirit measure for the kids – you'll need the distraction.

- An adjustable spanner to loosen nuts.

- Pliers, because the adjustable spanner never works.

- Four tools I bought in Aldi that I never use.

- A large collection of spare nuts and bolts from recent flatpack assemblies. They're not spare in the strictest sense of the word, but they were left over when I got to the end of the instructions. Hopefully they aren't essential.

Know the Drill

Our house is over sixty years old. The good thing about that is the walls aren't made with a mixture of air, glue and very light sticks. The downside is it can be very hard to drill a hole in an old brick wall. Those cheap, cordless drills you see on special offer are basically electric screwdrivers with delusions of grandeur. Nobody told me that, and I ended up spending four hours failing to put up TV brackets. The only thing I had to show for it were the four new curses that I invented.

If you plan to drill a hole in brick or stone, you can get a hammer-action device starting for about €70. I bought one once when planning to hang a curtain rail. The wrongly-aligned holes are still in the wall at our place, if you want a look. While you're there, you might like to buy a hammer-action drill, hardly ever used, because it was banned by the wife. (I can hardly blame her.)

Flatpack

There are two kinds of flatpack assembly – Before Child and After Child.

Before Child flatpack is where you take three hours to put together a chest of drawers, even though it said ninety minutes on the box.

After Child flatpack is where you try to sell your kids on the Internet, after one of them runs into the room where you are doing the assembly and kicks the box holding the twelve M8 screws.

Here's the bottom line. Flatpack assembly is stressful enough, without shouting 'get out of the room' every five minutes and trying to finish the job with only eleven M8 screws. The only way to do this is to tell your partner to take the kids out for five hours minimum because you know how these things can over-run. That way you should have two hours of kids-free time at the end to admire your handiwork. Or just take a lie down.

Don't suggest that 'Bradley' might like to do it. Paying a gorgeous handyman to assemble a chest of drawers is the point where your status goes from 'useless' to 'recently divorced'.

The Builder Provider's Store

A DIY store like B&Q or Woodies is grand if you need a screwdriver, or a hammer, or a 3D white plastic sign bearing the letters LOVE. After that, you're on to the 'hard' stuff. By which I mean a Builder Provider's store. It's hard because of the men behind the counter.

They have no time for DIY newbies. Going in there to ask

for advice on a Rawlplug is like trying to get the attention of a Parisian waiter using Junior Cert French. (If you don't know what a Rawlplug is, I wouldn't even bother leaving the house.)

I usually bring a savvy in-law to translate when I go into these places. That's not as odd as it sounds. You'll find a lot of people go there in pairs, more for support than anything else.

Electrics

There is a black patch on the wall of a rented house in Dublin. It's like a memorial for the one and only time I tried to wire a plug. It's funny how a loud bang and a burning smell would put you off touching electric wiring ever again.

Plumbing

Here is the vital question. Do you know where the stop-cock is for the mains in your house?

A: Yes.

B: No.

C: I thought stop-cock was a form of contraception?

If you answered B or C, I would step away from plumbing completely. Even if you answered A, I would check that your house insurance covers floods, before messing with running water. That might be the best advice I've given in this entire book.

3.10 YOUR HEALTH MATTERS

Yes, it's terrible when your kids get sick. But not as bad as when you get sick and have to look after them. Luckily, women are very understanding when their partners are feeling under the weather, said no man who ever woke one morning and told his wife he has the flu.

Seriously, guys, I fully believe that you have the flu. I'd drop you over a bottle of Lucozade, but my sinuses are a bit blocked at the moment and I'm trying to avoid going out.

The reality is that kids bring a lot of new things into your life, including new and angry viruses that they pick up at the crèche. I found that the most virulent stuff happened when they were about two or three, so I decided to write about it here.

As I write this, all four of us have been passing around a sinus thing for the last few months. Not even a true hypochondriac could claim it was the flu, but it actually might be easier if it was, because I could take to the bed and get rid of it. Anyway, you don't want to be listening to me complaining about my health issues. (No one does, as it turns out.)

Here's a sample of the health-related issues I've encountered since the kids arrived.

Man Flu

Get over it. There's a child in the house. No one wants to hear you say, 'I think I might be dying' in a slightly hoarse voice. There's nothing more to say here.

Dr Google

Dr Google is your friend. Not to give a valid diagnosis of your child's runny nose, because she'll end up having everything from a cold to the Black Death. The point of Dr Google is to stay abreast of what your partner is reading about your child's health. There is usually a test at the end and you better you know what you're talking about. Unless you are a big fan of the phrase, 'Maybe you should try a bit of parenting sometimes.'

So where can you get something that approximates to actual medical advice? I usually head for the NHS website. I can't guarantee that it will stay around forever, because the Tory Party would probably like to close it down, or hand it over to a deserving billionaire. Alternatively, you could always head for the Open University website and do a medical degree online. It beats getting online advice from Healing Hank in Alabama, who reckons that milk thistle is better than penicillin.

I feel sorry for the current generation of babies though. They are growing up with the Internet. By which I mean being held up next to an iPad screen, so their parents can compare them to a photo of a child with a rash on some website called WhoNeedsaDoctor.com. Seriously, that can't be good for their health.

The Chicken Pox Party

Seriously, it's a thing, where you bring your kids to a house where a child has chicken pox, so they can catch their dose and get it over and done with.

It's also a sign of how things have gone in your life. Remember your single years, when you'd go to a party and wouldn't mind catching something off someone, as long as you had a good time. Happy days.

I have no idea if it's a good idea to give your kids the pox. I just looked to the Internet there for some guidance and discovered some very angry people arguing about it.

Here is what I do know about chicken pox. It could ruin your holidays. So, if you already have a week in France booked for July and your kids get invited to a convenient chicken pox party in April, I'd invite you to draw your own conclusions. I'm not going to draw those for you, because I don't want to attract the attention of angry 'health experts' on the Internet. (You'd think with all that 'expertise', they could prescribe themselves with some kind of cure for their anger.)

I should add, in case you haven't noticed, that I'm not a doctor and I don't pretend to be one. So consult one if you want an actual proper opinion. (The lawyers wrote that last bit. They're very good at their job, so don't bother suing me or the publishers.)

In the meantime, I'm going to open a disease-spreading centre where you can drop the kids off for a couple of hours. It will be called InfectaKids. Or maybe just The Crèche.

The Free GP Card

The good news is your child is entitled to free GP visits up to the age of six. (At least this is the case in Ireland.) The bad news is you might be reluctant to take advantage. This is because you suffer from a common condition in Ireland, known as Mortophobia. The main symptom is a reluctance to take something free, in case people think you are taking the piss. You'd be morto if people thought that.

The real dread is that your child miraculously recovers on the way to the doctor's surgery and you end up wasting her valuable time. Don't worry, that isn't going to happen. Yes, the child might have been perfectly okay when she walked in the door of the doctor's surgery. At which point she stepped into the waiting room and picked up something from one of the little kids in there with snots hanging down to their knees. It's like a germ supermarket in there.

So, bring your child to the doctor if you are worried that something is amiss. If nothing else, you can always slip in a mention of your man flu, just as the doctor is finishing her examination. Not that she'll be able to do anything for you. But it's nice to have one person listening to your complaints. Particularly when the government is kind enough to pick up the bill.

4

THREENAGER

By year four, you should be getting good at the fatherhood thing. Or at least you would be if the goalposts didn't keep shifting.

A friend of mine once told me the key to parenting is to remember that everything is a phase, and he's got a point. By the time you are really good at changing nappies, they won't need them any more. Just when you get a knack for making puréed food, the little tykes go and grow a set of teeth. Those hours walking around trying to wind them on your shoulder, well they just seem like an awful waste of time.

So what's in store as your child hits three? Well, first of all, your two-year-old is now on the way to being a Threenager. That's a tricky business in itself. This is also the time for potty training. We've had mixed success with our two kids, mainly because we started the older one too early, as if it was some kind of competition.

This is also the time when you need to up your game on the discipline front or the kids will just take over the house. At last it's safe to bring them to a restaurant, as long as you know what you're doing. And you should get ready for the questions. Lots and lots of questions. Let's start with the Threenager and take it from there.

4.1 WELCOME TO YOUR THREENAGER

What's a Threenager?

A Threenager is a surprise. Remember the three little words that kept you going through the Terrible Twos – It. Will. Pass. That's what you said when your toddler's head nearly spun off because they had the wrong type of custard creams in Aldi. That's what you repeated when she cried extra hard in Nandos and almost set off the fire alarm.

It will pass. Your little girl will come through this and come out the other side as a little angel. This should last until about the age of nine, at which time all bets are off. I'll take that, says you, I could do with seven years of angel.

And then, soon after her third birthday, your promised angel wakes up one morning and greets the day with, 'I'm bored.' What? How could you be bored?

Welcome to your Threenager.

The Negotiations

Biddable. That's the word people like to use about the post-toddler brigade. There is no point in trying to negotiate with a toddler. Your best bet is to keep firing rice cakes at them until they hit the age of three. At which point they will be biddable. At least that's what you are told by people who have been through it.

These people are not wrong. It is possible to negotiate with a Threenager. The problem is that a three-year-old is a much better negotiator than you are. It's like they did some kind of business degree over the Internet and can get almost anything they want through the art of negotiation. As a result, you end up boasting that you only gave three chocolate fingers to your Threenager. 'Three?' says your partner, wondering where it all went wrong. 'Yeah, but he asked me for six of them and a helicopter,' you reply, realising how stupid that sounds once you say the words out loud.

The Iron Baby

There are only two things guaranteed to calm down a two-year-old – one episode of *Peppa Pig*, followed by another episode of *Peppa Pig*. This gives her ten minutes to come back down from The Crazy Place, while you get to look up 'sedatives for kids' on your phone. It's a time out for everyone. The problem with all that Peppa is, by the time she gets to three, your daughter has a *Made in Chelsea* accent that she uses to boss you around all day, because that's what Threenagers do for a living. Someone bossing you around in a cut-glass English accent – that sounds familiar. And then it dawns on you. You're sharing a house with Maggie Thatcher crossed with Theresa May. It's as weird as it sounds.

LazyTown

You'll miss *Peppa Pig* though. Never mind that Daddy Pig seems to have all the intelligence of a cheap vacuum cleaner. (It hopefully means your kids will underestimate you as they grow up. That's got to be a good thing. You'll take any advantage going.) At least *Peppa Pig* was written so that parents could have a laugh as well. (Particularly at Pedro Pony. We love his work.) *Peppa* means you can enjoy quality time with your child *and* watch TV. What a result.

Until your Threenager grows out of it and wants to watch *LazyTown*. You won't want to watch *LazyTown* with your child. Unless you want to spend half an hour every day despairing for the future of mankind. It's that bad and you should prepare for things to get worse. The next step for your Threenager is to show an interest in those zany, high-school Disney comedies where all the actors are in their early twenties. There's only one solution to that. A second telly.

Do You Remember?

Here is the golden rule of Threenagers. They are never wrong about anything. That isn't something they think about themselves. It is an actual fact. Worse again, it is an actual fact that makes you feel like you are losing your mind. Which of course you are. Twelve hours parenting every day for the last two years means everything is lost, all the time. Your brain is so over-loaded that you're afraid to think about dinner in case you forget how to drive. Your Threenager, on the other hand, forgets nothing. It's why they say 'do you remember' all the time.

This brings us to the second golden rule of Threenagers – never promise anything you can't deliver in the hope that they will forget about it when the time comes around. Not unless you want to be the first person sued by a three-year-old for breach of contract. Don't worry, there's an upside. Your hawk-like Threenager never misses a thing. So, go on, ask him where you left your car keys. Because he knows. And, let's face it, you don't.

This Shit is Real

One minute she's singing 'Twinkle, Twinkle, Little Star'. The next, it's 'All About that Bass'. There is nothing in between. In fairness, you taught her to sing 'All About that Bass' so your friends would get a great laugh when she sings the line, 'We know that shit ain't real'. (Oh look, she curses, just like her dad.)

But it's still a bit off-putting when a three-year-old asks you to move the dial on the radio because a song is boring. Particularly when that song is Taylor Swift's 'Shake it Off'. What, she's outgrown that already? Yes. It's like she skipped from age two to seven overnight. That's Threenagers for you.

They Know What They Like

Particularly when it comes to clothes. If you think boys are inclined to wear anything, then you should have seen the face on my little guy when he woke up one morning and decided he'd had enough of Spider-Man. There goes a whole drawer of long-sleeve tops, said we, trudging off to the clothes shop. Still, in fairness to him, at least he tended to pick and stick with outfits for more than a couple of hours.

His sister had a more short-term window. I've never been to a Lady Gaga concert, but I hear she does a costume change every half an hour. That's quite a long time in one outfit compared to you, my little lady. This could develop into a full-blown nightmare if her mom was away overnight and I was left in charge of outfit selection.

You can read about it in my next book, *Three-Year-Old Girls are Very Unpredictable*. Here is a quick summary. My daughter and I agreed on an acceptable top and leggings combo for the next morning, just before I sang her to sleep. So far, so Capable Dad. In the middle of the night, the Evil Toddler Fairies came and replaced my daughter with a very similar-looking, but actually entirely different child. Which is why she woke up the next morning and asked me to dress her in the Elsa dress with curly tights. No, I didn't know what she meant either. Obviously, I couldn't ring my wife and ask for any pointers because that's the kind of 'men are useless story' that tends to get legs on Facebook. (Ah look at the poor man, he hasn't a clue.)

So off we went through my daughter's wardrobe for a game of 'Is This What You Mean?' I never knew she had so many clothes. Or that she could change her mind twenty-seven times during the game of 'Is This What You Mean?' I got a crash course in her outfits when the wife returned home. I'd recommend you do the same, so you are ready to dress her when the time comes. Because, let's just say, three-year-old girls are very good at crying out loud at their stupid daddy.

4.2 OH BOY

A lot of my original Threenager knowledge was based on our three-year-old girl. I thought the lessons learned there would come in handy when our son headed out of toddlerdom. I thought wrong. Despite what people might tell you, boys are different to girls.

Here are some of the key differences I spotted as number two headed into his third year.

Funny Farts

The father–son bond doesn't really get going until you share a good laugh over a fart. After that, it's like you're one person. He will be delighted to find someone with the same sense of humour. So will you.

His mother likes to discourage this because, as we know, she never farts herself. But you understand where he is coming from. In later life he will explain his love of farting as an evolutionary thing, something we used to scare away wild animals back when we all lived in caves. This is something we invented so that women won't think we're morons. The truth is, we haven't a clue why we like farting. But we do. And nobody likes it more than a three-year-old boy. (Except maybe his dad.)

Is He Full Yet?

You know that food you are giving him? It isn't enough. That extra snack to keep him away from the fridge? That isn't enough either. The most popular sentence among parents of three-year-old boys is, 'Are you absolutely sure he hasn't got worms?'

The second most popular is, 'Do you think we can get some kind of grant? This human cookie monster is costing us a fortune.' The third is the most important of all. 'No way, it's your turn. His nappy yesterday was like something from a horror movie. I actually had a nightmare about it.'

Ouch, That Really Hurts

There is a good chance his first words will be 'Jesus, that hurts.'

There is every chance he'll learn this phrase from you. The minute your little guy hits eighteen months, he'll start hitting you. Once he gets to the age of three, it will start to hurt.

His favourite move is where he takes a run-up and head-butts your thigh. Two inches higher and you'd be talking about a homemade vasectomy. (If you could talk.) The bad news is you're a man and not allowed to complain about pain. The even worse news is that toddlers often grow two inches overnight. So now might be a good time to buy one of those jockstraps that cricket players use for their crown jewels.

Roar!

One episode of *Peppa Pig* is like a guide video to little boys. Peppa's little brother George is basically your son, but with a posher accent. (Unless you live in south County Dublin.) George has one answer to everything – dinosaurs. Likewise, your little guy can sit for hours, going 'ROAR!' with his toy dinosaurs. Don't worry, there is nothing wrong with this carry on, even if his older sister was playing the piano by this age. And remember, every minute he's lost in Dinosaur World is a minute where he isn't running head-first into your thigh.

By the way, the more progressive parents out there might decide to buy their guy a doll. In my experience, she quickly becomes a Dollysaurus and is soon ROARING! away with the rest of them.

He's Going Bananas

Here is a business opportunity for you. Toddler Boy Tantrum Energy.

Here is how it works. You start peeling his banana even though you know it makes him furious, because he wants to do it himself, what with him being a big boy. This drives him nuts. You hook him up to the national grid. He powers the town of Athlone.

So yes, the tantrums can have a certain power to them. But they are not as bad as your little girl's tantrums. You know, the three-hour affairs where you wear wellies indoors because the floor is covered in tears. A toddler boy is easily distracted out of a tantrum. Try a dinosaur. If that fails, go for a fart.

The Hair
There will come a time when you'll have to cut his hair. Before that, you get to enjoy Name that Rock Star. That's where you get to try to figure out which rock star he looks like with his mad hair. It's more entertaining than it sounds. (It would want to be, says you.)

The hair will cause trouble in the end though. Despite the fact that your son looks like a young Jon Bon Jovi, there is a voice in your head saying, 'Would you ever take that young fella away and get his hair cut, he looks like a shagging girl?' That voice is, of course, your own dad. You'll be hearing more and more from Inner Dad Voice over the next few years. And then you'll wake up one day and discover you have, in fact, become your own dad. It can be hard to take.

The Big Boy
Fancy a cheap laugh from your toddler? Call him a baby. And then run for it. He's a big boy, okay, a big boy. And you're

cruising for a dead leg. Here is the difference between three-year-old girls and boys. A three-year-old girl is fascinated that she was once a baby, and would like to go back to being one so she could look after herself. Boys are embarrassed by their baby years. Babies can't talk, aren't strong and don't even laugh at farts. 'I'm not a baby, you are. ROAR!' says he, closing in on your thigh.

The Smelly Pony

It's traditional for little girls to ask their parents for a pony. Here's my advice. Give them a little brother. (They're slightly cheaper.) You'd have to look closely to see the difference between a pony and a three-year-old boy. Both are fully capable of running around in a circle all day. They're kind of smelly. And more than anything else, they're great fun. You see, that's the main thing about three-year-old boys. You might never stop laughing.

4.3 THE BEDTIME STORY

Your bedtime routine changes over the years. Up to their first birthday they were often breastfed to sleep and my job was to sit there and do nothing. This isn't as good as it sounds. Because this makes you the perfect choice when it comes to putting them to bed without a helping boob in site. Actually, I think men are good at this; we can be fairly hard-nosed in terms of putting kids into bed and scooting out the door. (Or 'heartless' as my wife likes to call it.)

This is all just a phoney war, though. The real challenge is when you have to calm down a toddler or child enough to get them into pyjamas and then into bed. Let's just say they mightn't want to. Like every other couple out there, we plodded through it until we found what works. So, here's what worked for us, as the kids moved from age two to four.

Timing is Everything

Obviously, it varies depending on their age and how many box sets you plan to watch before going to bed yourself. Our two, aged three and five, go at 7.30 p.m. This gives us two hours of adult time, by which I mean stuffing our faces with chocolate and two episodes of *Game of Thrones*. (Or *Made in Chelsea*, if we fancy something less realistic.)

A word for those who think that if you keep them up for an hour, they'll give you an extra hour in bed the following morning. The word is 'sorry'. It doesn't work like that. Mess with their bedtime and anything could happen. Except for that morning sex you had planned, because your son still bounced into your bedroom at 6.30 the next morning. But we put him to bed an hour late, says you, wondering if you'd get more action by joining the monks.

The Routine

It seems to me that kids will go along with anything, as long as they are expecting it to happen. We read books and have a chat every night and they head for the room fairly willingly. But if we slaughtered a little goat at 7.15 every night, they'd probably also see that as a sign that it's time for bed. (As long as they didn't get too attached to the little goat.)

So figure out what works for you. And, if you have a boy,

stick to it. From what I've seen and heard, boys are sticklers for detail. Which is a nice way of saying, if things aren't just so at bedtime, your little Jack will do his nut.

Once the story and chat is over, our little boy has to be lifted to the bedroom, where he lists out the colours of the letters of his name on the door, getting each one wrong deliberately. Then he turns the light on, off, on, off, on and off again. Then he is ready for bed. Any deviation and he goes bananas. The problem is he doesn't go bananas there and then; he waits until you are just about ready to eat that first bar of chocolate. That's a heartbreaker. So stick with the routine.

Sing Out Loud

Don't ask me why, but the sound of me croaking my way through 'Edelweiss' every night tends to reassure the kids. If I tried it outside the house, I'd probably be issued with a barring order.

Another popular request at bedtime is the song they sing at the end of *In The Night Garden* on CBeebies. It's one of those songs you can sing even if you don't have a note in your head, like 'The Fields of Athenry'. That's the end of my song repertoire, except for a few Pulp songs, and it would look weird if I stood there singing 'Sorted for E's and Wizz' to my kids.

At this point I leave the room, leaving my wife to sing a final song about dinosaurs while I take the secret chocolate stash out of hiding. This is where the day starts for me, really.

Bath Time?

I'd say American kids must be very clean. All those American parenting sites with 'Five things to help baby sleep' articles say you should give them a bath every night. They usually come with a photo of a baby sitting in the bath, while his hot mother smiles at him with a few suds on her perfect nose. (I'd say she's had work done.) There is often a hipster dad in the photo as well, looking very pleased with himself.

Maybe that is how bath-time works on the other side of the Atlantic. Maybe the children there don't get soap in their eyes or wriggle like crazy and have a conniption when it's time to rinse their hair. Or maybe this is all a myth to sell expensive shower gel for kids.

We give ours a bath once a week, whether they need it or not. Their mother does all the hard work, with a carefully honed shower routine that doesn't end in tears, involving ducks and dinosaurs that must be washed as well. It all works nicely and they are fit for human company for another week. (Unless one of them gets the runs, in which case they get a quick hose down just in case.)

The Hour Change

Here is what I know about people who say the hour going forward doesn't affect their life – they don't have kids. We worked hard over one winter to establish a routine that had our kids in bed for 7 p.m. And then the hour went forward.

So 7 p.m is really only 6 p.m., as far as they are concerned. Confusing, isn't it. Try and explain it to a crazed toddler at 9 p.m., which is really 8 p.m., from where he's bouncing.

At least he won't wake until 8 a.m. tomorrow morning, says you, not thinking it through. Because then October rolls around and the hour goes back again. So now, your child, who had got used to going to bed at 7.30 p.m. during the summer, wants to hit the sack at 6.30. (If he doesn't hit the sack, he'll hit you.) That's good – it gives you an extra hour of chocolate and Facebook. What isn't good is 6 a.m. the next morning, which is 7 a.m. in crazed toddler real time. That's the time he gets up. As they say on *Game of Thrones*, 'winter is coming'.

Keep it Down

They should make a horror movie about 7.40 p.m. in our house. It would be called *I Think They've Gone to Sleep*.

It's like this. If they get through the next five minutes without shouting 'I can't find Ducky', they'll probably sleep all night. The tension is unbearable. I've developed this new, ultra-silent version of shallow breathing, like they probably used in *Alien* when the creature was two feet away. Sometimes I don't get enough oxygen and nearly pass out, but it's worth it if they drift off to dreamland.

The key is to make it through that fifteen minutes after they go down. Then you can make as much noise as you like. We live right next to Cork City's football ground, which lets out a fair roar for a home goal. This doesn't wake them. Neither does the annoying guy on the PA system reading out the same long-winded message every week about respecting local residents on the way home. Once the kids are gone, they're gone. As long as you don't make too much noise opening a bag of crisps. You'd be surprised how that can burrow into a sleeping child's ear and whisper, 'Wake up, wake up, you're missing out on crisps.'

You're Up

It doesn't always work like that. Sometimes they wake up an hour after going to bed, particularly if they think you are enjoying yourself. This kicks off a game of 'Pretending Not To Hear Them In The Hope That My Partner Will Go In'.

Here's how that pans out. You take out your phone and pretend to read something on Facebook. Your wife says, 'Are you not going to go and see what's wrong?' You say, 'I went the last time.' She says, 'I went the two times before that and anyway I had to push them out in the maternity hospital.' You say, 'It's not my fault you're the one with the womb.'

The good news is that by now your child has probably stopped crying. The bad news is your wife hates you and there's no sex for a week. So, here's my advice. The second you hear a murmur from the kids, take out your phone and set the timer to five minutes. There is to be no talking or going into the child during this time, unless you suspect there might be a fire. Nine times out of ten, the child will be back asleep when the five minutes is up. And you're still on speaking terms.

4.4 IT'S POTTY TIME

We had mixed results with potty training. As I said earlier, I reckon we started too early with our eldest, and ended up with months of soaking underwear in a bucket, tears, regression and frayed nerves. As a result, we put off training our little guy until he hit three and he pretty much trained himself in half an hour.

Here's the thing. I'm no expert, but nappies aren't so big

a hassle that you need to rush into potty training. The only urgency is when they hit three and are entitled to free pre-school, as long as they are out of nappies. You don't want to miss out on that.

But the reality is they will probably let you know they are ready for training before that, by holding on to it, or telling you that it's happening right now, in their nappy. (It's cuter than you'd think.)

My top tip would be to spend a week showing them Elmo potty-training videos on YouTube before kicking it all off. And try to bite your tongue when they wet themselves five times in a row. As my aunt used to say, they won't still be doing that when they are twenty-one. (Hopefully, anyway.)

Here's a look at some of the things we encountered when potty training the kids.

The Book

The go-to book is Gina Ford's *Potty Training in One Week*. This sounds as optimistic as 'Get your Two-Year-Old to Dress Himself Using Praise and Cooing Sounds'.

That said, it is practical and clear and not overly optimistic, given how long it took our younger fella. We are actually thinking of putting up a bronze statue of him in the back garden. His big sister is upset with all the attention he got, but he is definitely our favourite now. (Only messing, Freda. And well done for learning to read.)

Here's the main thing that dads need to know about Gina Ford's book. You won't read it, despite swearing blind that you will. There doesn't seem to be anything anyone can do about this. I've read a bit of it for this book, so feel free to quote me like a boss.

When to Start?

The whole potty training arena can be very competitive. Gina Ford reckons a child should be ready for potty training from the age of eighteen months. There is no point in arguing about this, because Gina Ford has sold a squillion books and I haven't. Bear in mind that all your partner's friends will have the same idea when they read the book: I can do better than that. That's why you'll find women showing Elmo's 'Potty Time' video to their four-hour-old baby in the maternity hospital. Like I say, competitive.

As a dad, your main job will be soaking small, wet underpants every night, because your eighteen-month-old didn't quite get what was going on in the *Bear in the Big Blue Mountain* potty training video. The good news is she can sing every note of the weird rap in that video (look it up on YouTube); the bad news is she often does this while wetting herself.

You Put Your Botty on the What?

The Elmo and *Bear in the Big Blue Mountain* songs work a treat, as long as the child is old enough. They are simple, addictive songs that seem to get into their heads. The problem is, they'll also get into your head. Which is fine until you drift a bit during an important meeting at work and suddenly blurt out, 'You do the poo poo that you do so well.' With any luck your boss will have kids and might even join in. Otherwise, I hear LinkedIn is the best way to find a new job.

When is the Best Time to Do It?

Gina Ford says the best time to take on potty training is during the summer, when it's dry and the child can spend most of its time outside. She's obviously never been to Ireland. But soaking dirty underpants in a bucket is slightly more palatable when it isn't freezing cold outside. Which, in Ireland, is from mid-July to late July. There's your window of opportunity.

Reward Charts

We had some success with reward charts for our daughter. They're cards with, say, twenty spaces for stickers, and you add a sticker after every successful visit to the potty. A row of stickers earns a small treat; a full card earns a bigger treat. Just to be clear, the treat is for the child. Toilet training is tough for parents, but there's no need to award yourself with a weekend in Bordeaux just because your child filled a chart.

Don't make the treat too good. Otherwise your toddler will move into the jacks full-time, sitting there purple-faced trying to push something out. It can be a bit off-putting when you are trying to have a shower.

The harsher side of reward charts is that you remove a sticker after every 'accident'. I'm not sure this does much for the child, but it gave me some satisfaction before I set about clearing up the mess. (I never said I wasn't petty.)

I'm Finished!

That means she did a poo and needs someone to come in and wipe her bum. (There's another thing you didn't think about before you had children.)

Some people are weird about wiping someone else's bum. The alternative is you insist that she wipes her own bum. Go that route if you enjoy dealing with a child who has half a roll of toilet-paper stuck to her bum and looks like she is about to start a dirty protest. Otherwise wipe away until they are coming up to school age. (They don't have someone to wipe their bums in school. I checked.)

Water, Water Everywhere

Just because you don't wash your hands after going to the toilet doesn't mean you should pass that habit on to your kids. The bit they don't tell you in potty training school is that you will also need to teach kids how to wash their hands. The good news is it's very easy to get a child to start washing his hands. The bad news is that it's virtually impossible to get him to stop.

It's as if one of the Ten Commandments for kids reads, 'Thou shalt never willingly step away from running water.' Bear that in mind as you bask in the glow of a child doing his first poo in the potty. You are now going to have to spend ten minutes trying to lure him away from the sink. And then another five minutes mopping the bathroom floor. (Kids are very splashy.)

Do You Need to Go?

The five words that dominate your life after the nappy comes off – 'Do you need to go?' There is an urge to check a nappy-less child every ten minutes. This gap drops to every five minutes after you've cleared up your first poo-related accident.

No one is going to judge you for that, it's a messy business. But look at it this way – how would you feel if someone came up to you every five minutes and said, 'Do you need to go?' The answer would be, 'Yes, I need to go to another family, please leave me alone.' So maybe step away from the child and let them make their own mistakes for a while.

Night Training

The final step is to take the nappy off at night. Views seem to differ on when a child is ready for this. Gina Ford reckons the child should be three, and have dry, or nearly dry, nappies in the morning, for a few weeks. I've heard others say you're good to go after three dry morning nappies.

All I'll say is that it's a good idea to put replacement sheets and pyjamas near their bed, so you won't go bananas trying to find them at 3 a.m. in the morning after an accident. Let's just say your patience levels might be somewhere between 'livid' and 'angry crocodile'. There's no way you want to lay that on your child.

Daaaaad – Stop!

I'm still congratulating our five-year-old when she goes, even though she hasn't had an accident since forever. It's like I'm afraid to stop with the praise in case I jinx it and she ends up back in nappies. But I guess I'd better stop at some stage. Otherwise I'll just end up at her twenty-first birthday, praising her in front of her friends for doing her wees. That's not a great look.

4.5 HOW'S YOUR DISCIPLINE?

As I said above, at least when they hit three, they're biddable. Trying to impose discipline on a young toddler is like trying to catch a goldfish with a spoon. Now they're in their fourth year, there is some chance you can shape their behaviour with threats, incentives, cash, chocolate and back-to-back movies with Maltesers. (Don't judge me until you have been there yourself.)

There's no shortage of literature and advice about discipline. I'd be wary about telling you how to manage it with your kids; we're all different.

What I'm offering here is a sideways glance at what did and didn't work in our house. If nothing else it might give you some food for thought.

Time Out

Here's the thing. It isn't a time out if they follow you around the house shouting, 'But I don't want to sit at the bottom of the stairs.' The trick is to get them to stay put. I know what you're thinking. But a set of restraints in the front room will only give the wrong impression. Particularly to those people who can't resist saying, 'I see the arrival of the kids has done nothing to dampen your sex life.' (Seriously?)

Your only option is to keep a cot on the go until the youngest child reaches five. It's like a prison, without the barbed wire. Try to resist the temptation to put barbed wire on the edge if they escape during time outs. It's all fun and games and then you get a visit from the Public Health Nurse.

Reward Charts

The same one I mentioned a few pages back in the potty-training section can also be used to reward good behaviour. Or at least that's the theory. Here's the reality:

Me: 'I'll put another sticker on your chart if you do it.'

Child: 'How many more stickers do I need before a treat?'

Me: 'Seven.'

Child: 'I'd need something quicker than that, to be honest. We're talking a bar of chocolate in the next thirty seconds.'

Shouting

Why shouldn't you shout at your kids? They shout at you, all the time. In fact, not shouting at your kids now and again is bad for everyone involved. You'll just store up the anger and end up shouting at your partner, who will move to Madrid with the au pair. Your child will end up traumatised the first time someone shouts at her for real and will probably end up suing you when she's twenty-one. (That's the way the world is going now.)

You Have Until Five

We've all been there. 'If you don't come over here before I count to five, I'm going to leave you here in this playground/shop/place you didn't seem to really enjoy but now you don't want to leave. I should have listened to my sister and never had kids.'

There seems to be a notion out there that the child will come running, even though this has never actually happened in real life. What actually happens is you get to five and then walk towards them like an eejit. This is where they start to run away and it becomes clear why you shouldn't have waited until your mid-thirties to have a child. In short, the only way to get a child to leave a playground is to sneak up behind them and bribe them with a lollipop. Anything else will result in tears.

Electronics Ban

The good news is that banning access to phones, tablets and games consoles is one of the most effective deterrents you can use on a brazen child. The bad news is your children will have no idea how to entertain themselves and will follow you around for the duration of the ban. Who knew that someone could repeat 'I'm bored' for four hours solid? Not you, because you locked them in their room for the duration of the ban. Come on, it's punishment. You're allowed to be a little cruel.

Tidy Up

Your children aren't always going to wreck your house. It turns out they take a break between the ages of four and sixteen, at which point they'll start having parties behind your back. (It's not like you didn't do it yourself.)

Anyway, the threat of getting them to tidy up their mess might be a useful way to keep the under-fours onside. That is, if you have the patience to watch them trying to get four pieces of Lego into a box. Which you don't, because three hours is a long time. So steer clear of the tidy up threat. Because the child knows what it means. 'Stop that now or I'll force you to sit there while I tidy up the house, because you are really good at pretending to daydream just to see if you can drive me mental.'

Food

There is a good chance you are already punishing your kids with food without realising it. You know, giving them kale smoothies just so you can look like Super Dad in front of your friends. But have you ever considered actively using food as a deterrent?

'One more word out of you and we'll be having boiled kidney stew for tea,' that sort of thing. Anyone who reckons that isn't a deterrent never had boiled kidney stew for tea. Obviously, your child will pretend to like this vomit on a plate, just to get on your wick. This is why I recommend kidney stew for the bold child, served alongside pizza, chips and a Viennetta per person for everyone else. Now that's what I call discipline.

Empty Threats

'I'm warning you, once more and your monster truck is go-ing in the bin,' says you in despair, because everyone involved in this sad charade knows that's never going to happen. If the monster truck ever makes it to the bin, then your child will throw a wobbler that will have the neighbours ringing social services. So you make things worse by downgrading the threat. 'Okay, that's it now, I'm going to put your truck up on the fridge. For an hour.'

At this stage, your Threenager would be feeling sorry for you, if he was capable of remorse. He isn't, so he carries on pulling the cat's tail, just to hear it squeal. You put the truck on the fridge. He pretends to be upset, because that's part of the game too, a game that he wins every time.

It's hard to stop this from happening. Throwing the truck in the bin will kick off a world of pain that could last for who knows how long? But it reminds me of something my father-in-law said: 'It's your job, as a parent, to always follow through on your threats.' I can't manage this, and my kids are probably well down the road to a life of crime.

Do as I What Now?

Finally, it's important that you set a good example for your child. Sorry about that. Here are a couple of skills you should develop. 1: The ability to eat a Magnum ice-cream in five seconds flat, in case your child walks into the room. 2: Use your internal voice when you are driving in case your child ends up thinking it's okay to call someone a f****** **** ** **, just because they indicated slightly late. 3: Try not to laugh at your own farts, even if it's a really, really funny one. That can be tricky.

4.6 CAN I ASK YOU A QUESTION, DAD?

I love the way my daughter asks permission to ask a question, before she goes on to ask the question. She's obviously picking up politeness from somewhere. And the questions (she's five, there are lots of questions) shine a light on what's going on in her head.

Once your child hits three, you are basically a contestant on a round-the-clock quiz show. It's not as cute as it sounds. Just as I love when Freda asks why our cat can't fly, I also love to be left alone for five minutes so I can stare out the window and enjoy a cup of tea. Some days you're tired, some days you're not.

That's why I have a deliberate resolution pasted inside my head – answer every question. As much as Selfish Me would like them to skive off and leave me alone for a few minutes, Proper Dad Me knows that they're not just looking for information when they ask a question. They are also asking me to focus on them alone, to give them my time of day. Built into every question is an implicit 'Do you love me?' I do, of course I do. So I try to answer every question with a smile on my face, even if I have no idea why sand is called sand. Because they'll stop asking questions soon enough and I don't want any regrets.

Below are some of the questions I faced in the last few years.

What Are You Eating?

I'm not sure when humans lose the ability to hear someone crunching a chocolate finger from up to 500 metres away. It's definitely after five years of age, because the easiest way to get my daughter in from the back garden is to take a mouse-like nibble on a biscuit. Sometimes I forget and she just appears at my side, as if we're in a horror movie called *Biscuit Girl 2*. She's learned that if she asks for one of these biscuits, I can just say 'no'. So now this is how the conversation goes:

'What are you eating?'

'Nothing.'

'Why are you chewing?'

'I'm not.'

'I'm going to stay here so you can't have another one.'

'Okay, here. Don't tell your brother.'

Where's Mom?

I wish I knew. That way I could send you over to her and I could finish reading this article about José Mourinho's new haircut. Younger kids need to know where their parents are at any given time. That's so cute. Particularly when you're the one they are looking for, because you're getting some down time in Vegas. 'I love my kids so much, when they're at home with their mother,' says you, force-feeding their education fund into a slot machine.

Do Snails Think They Are Going Fast?

And then there are the questions that make it all worthwhile, the ones where you realise you've been looking at the world like an adult for way too long. The other day, our five-year-old struck gold with this one, about snails. I haven't laughed so much since a nun came to our school in fifth year to give us marriage advice.

My daughter got the snail question from watching the movie *Turbo*. And they said kids will never learn anything from sitting in front of a screen.

For the record, I have no idea if snails think they are going fast. If you do, please get in touch, my daughter is still waiting for an answer. I'd like to say waiting patiently, but she's five.

Where Did I Come From?

Sitting them down to watch the movie *Storks* will only make things worse.

'How did the stork know where to bring the baby? Why do I look like Daddy? Why couldn't Santa do it?'

A lot of people reckon you should give your kids some sex facts before they discover them on the web. I'm happy for the Internet to take the strain on this one, if it means I don't have to introduce them to the term 'special hug'. It's all cute and nice now. But sometime soon they'll learn what special hug actually means and they'll mock you about it for the rest of your life. There's only one solution to that. Tell them to special hug off.

How Many Sleeps?

There is one thing that kids love even more than sugar or standing between you and the fridge. (We're thinking of getting a second fridge, to give us an option.)

And that one thing they love is the next thing. Your kids are basically event junkies. Once Christmas was over in our place, myself and the wife were hauled in for interrogation by our eldest, asking how long until spring/Easter/my birthday/my brother Joe's birthday/your birthday/the next time we can eat cake for breakfast. We tell her the number of sleeps to each one. If you think she won't ask again tomorrow, you've never had a five-year-old.

Do You Remember?

Soon after he discovers he has a nose and starts picking it for six months, your toddler will discover he has a memory.

Part of this discovery involves asking you if you remember everything that's in his lovely little head.

This memory is broken into two parts. The first part is everything that happened today. The second part is everything that happened in his life before that. Your child will call this yesterday. Prepare for questions like, 'Do you remember we went to Tesco yesterday because it was raining?' It's all cute really. Until he says, 'Do you remember when I used to sleep in a cot next to your bed, and you and Mom used to make that funny noise together in the middle of the night?' Oh oh.

Can I Get a Spaceship to Heaven?

It isn't a lost David Bowie song, but I can see where you are going. This is what happens when a much-loved grandparent passes away and you wheel out heaven to save the day. Never mind you didn't get them baptised and they have their names down in the Educate Together. Heaven explains everything, and it beats 'Life's a bitch and then you die', which can sound a bit harsh when you're three. (Not to mention forty-three.)

The answer to, 'Can I get a spaceship to heaven?' is, of course, 'No.' This led to a follow-up question in our house. 'Do Ryanair fly there?'

'No, they fly to a place called heaven-purgatory, and then you have to get a bus.' (If you're good.)

Will You Help Me Find My ...?

I can help, but we still won't find it. The first rule of having a Threenager is while they never forget a promise, or where you put your keys, they are incredibly good at losing their toys.

The second rule is you are in denial about your need to wear glasses – you'd struggle to find a haystack in a needle. Put these two rules together and you end up with a parent who is liable to burst into tears at the very mention of the word 'find'. (Try it with a parent you know. It's pretty funny the first few times.) In my experience, the best way to answer a 'will you help me find' question, is with another question. And that other question is, 'Would you like a chocolate finger?' Works every time.

4.7 THE RESTAURANT

As I said earlier on in the book, there is not much joy to be had in bringing a one- or two-year-old to a restaurant. It's okay when they are very young and liable to sleep. Or failing that, you can imprison them in the buggy with an unlimited supply of rice cakes. Once that option goes, you are dealing with a fired-up fidget who is far more likely to knock over a jug of water than eat anything on the menu. If you can sit through this and enjoy your own food, then you've obviously had your nerves surgically removed.

This changes around the thirty-month mark, when they are more biddable and likely to eat anything they can dip in ketchup. I love bringing them to restaurants now. As my grandfather always said, 'You have to get out and meet the people.' Eating out is a shared social occasion, a bit like Mom and Dad duck parading their young ones in front of other Mom and Dad ducks. Unless you insist on bringing your kids to a child-unfriendly restaurant, which is the kind of craziness that should preclude you from having kids in the first place.

Here's what you can expect when you start dining out with the little ones.

Deal or No Deal

You know how it goes.

'I'll have two cheeseburgers, nuggets, the spicy thing in the photo over there and two bottles of water.'

'Would you like to save money and turn that into a meal deal?'

'How does that work?'

'I talk really quickly, you say "yes" to everything because your kids are hungry and the whole thing ends up costing more.'

'Ahm, no, in that case.'

Drink!

You know how it goes.

'And what would you like to drink, sir?'

'Two glasses of red wine. And two for my wife. We're bringing them to the cinema and you don't want to do that with the kids unless you're half pissed.'

'And for the kids, sir?'

'Pasteurised tap water. We're not the type of parents who like to poison our kids with fruit juice. That stuff is full of sugar.'

'That stuff also distracts them so you can drink in peace, sir.'

'Give them four bottles of juice each. And more wine for myself and the missus. We're going to a sing-along *Frozen*. I don't want to remember a thing.'

The Foolish Foodies

You know how it goes.

'What would you like to eat kids?'

'Pizza and marshmallows.'

'What would happen if I brought you for some organic seafood in a Japanese noodle bar where they use seaweed instead of salt?'

'The same thing that happened the last time.'

'But you're three now. Surely you're too old to cry for thirty minutes solid, before taking a dump in your pants.'

'You'd think so, wouldn't you? Give us pizza and marshmallows, Dad. Anything else will end in tears and apologies. Japanese people are very understanding, but even they have their limits.'

The Guaranteed Thing that Will Happen

You mightn't know how it goes, not yet.

'I can't believe we managed to get out to a restaurant, honey. All those people who laughed and said our social life was toast once Sophie came along! And yet here we are in our favourite restaurant with our lovely daughter, surrounded by family and friends. She's eating risotto with truffles and basil and she's not even four yet. I'm so proud of her. And I'm so annoyed with all the people who say that kids wreck your life. Hang on, she's puking her guts up all over our favourite restaurant and it's green because of the basil. Jesus, she's still going, it's starting to flow around the floors now. How could so much puke come out of one little child? The waiter looks really cross. I'm going to cry.'

Latte?

You know how it goes.

'Do you think the kids will sit still and let us enjoy a coffee?'

'I'd says it's less likely than Donald Trump becoming a Muslim.'

'But look at them there, colouring away, surely nothing will stop them doing that for the next ten minutes. Waiter, we'll have two coffees please.'

Eldest child looks up. 'Dad, I'm really bored. I'm thinking of getting up and running around the restaurant, you'll try and catch me but it won't work and everyone will be looking at you.'

'Waiter, make those coffees to go. And make them Irish coffees while you're at it.'

High-chair

You know how it goes.

'Go over there and get him a high-chair, honey.'

'But he's three years of age.'

'All the more reason to restrain him in public.'

'You make a great point.' Gets chair.

Booth or Table?

You know how it goes.

'Would you like a booth or ordinary table, sir?'

'What's the difference?'

'Well, in the ordinary table area of our restaurant, people eat their meals while seated on a chair and then leave happy. Over in the booth area, a small child standing at the next booth will stare at you weirdly while you try to eat your meal. You'll have trouble sleeping for weeks.'

'Ordinary table it is then.'

Kiddies Menu

'Are you ready to order sir?'

'Yes. We'll have chips.'

'Anything else with that sir?'

'No, what's the point? They only ever eat the chips.'

'You're so right, sir.'

Head of Entertainment

'Dad, can I have your phone to look at a video please?'

'No, you cannot. We're going to sit here and have a conversation over dinner, like a normal family.'

'But every other kid here is watching a video on their father's phone while he downs another sneaky pint.'

Dad looks around restaurant. 'Okay, two conditions. Don't friend request some randomer on Facebook like you did the last time. And don't tell Mom.'

How Much?

'How much did it come to?'

'Thirty-seven euro.'

'But we shared two sandwiches, one portion of chips and drank tap water. How could it come to thirty-seven euro?'

'The food itself came to six euro and they added on thirty-one euro for something called "Because we are in Ireland".'

Hot Waitress

Waitress: 'I'll be right back with your drinks.' Hot waitress walks off.

Wife: 'Could you have flirted with her any more?'

You: 'I could have flirted with her all day if you and the kids weren't following me around, cramping my style.'

Wife: 'But she's half your age.'

You: 'You say that like it's a bad thing.'

4.8 SCHOOL TIME

I hated going back to school when I was small. Summer was getting up late and chips in the back seat of the car. School was getting up early and corned-beef sandwiches at a tiny desk.

It's not entirely different when you have kids. Yes, it comes as a relief in early September that someone else is going to entertain them, five mornings a week. But I'm also sad to say goodbye to another summer and pack the kids off to school. Mainly because our recent summers have also been about getting up a bit later and eating chips in the car; except this time I'm sitting in front.

Here's a quick survival guide, so your life doesn't go off the rails when September rolls around.

The Tears

It's not unusual to see a playground full of parents crying their eyes out, weeping tears of unbridled joy because now it's someone else's job to entertain their ungrateful kids. Under no circumstances should you make a sly quip to the teacher about their two-month holiday. The last thing you need now is for one of them to get the hump and go out on strike.

Holiday Bragging

There's nothing like meeting other parents in the first few weeks back and hearing their holidays weren't as good as yours. Bear in mind this is Ireland, so make sure to play down any enjoyment you had in case people think you are a bit up yourself. Also insist you booked it last minute, for next to nothing. The last thing you need is word going around that you're loaded or the principal will be on the phone asking for a 'voluntary contribution'. (The roof is leaking again.)

Traffic

There is only one thing worse than the back-to-school traffic in the mornings. And that's the person who insists on talking about it.

'The traffic is murder in the mornings now, isn't it?'

'It is.'

'Imagine what it will be like when it gets a bit darker.'

'I know.'

'It took me forty-five minutes to get from Douglas into town.'

'Really?'

'Bumper to bumper the whole way, I was half bored to death.'

'I know the feeling.'

Good Morning?

Not really. There are many words that capture a morning

where both kids are missing a shoe – good isn't one of them. 'Very' and 'bad' are two words that come to mind. 'Just like yesterday' would work as well. Sorry to be the bearer of bad news. That one-hour summer bonus snooze is in the bin. Get up out of bed early and start looking for those shoes.

Lunch

Here is how lunch works. If you give your kids something they really like (i.e. crisps or chocolate) all the other kids will go home and tell their parents that they want it too. As revenge for all the grief, these parents will then report you to the department for poisoning your kids with Hula Hoops. There is a lot of hysteria around food now, which means this is on a par with accusations of witchcraft in the Middle Ages. So, stay safe and give them the kind of lunch you'd expect to get from a hippy. (You can't go wrong with rye bread. They use that as a punishment in prison.)

The Expense

A survey last year found it costs almost €1,000 a year to send a child to primary school, rising to €1,500 for secondary. Make sure to grumble about this in public, in case the principal thinks you are made of money. (See above on voluntary contributions.) Even though it's actually a bargain, considering they look after your kids for most of the year and they teach them stuff as well.

Homework

Helping them with homework is a drag. It's hard, trying to

read an Irish book about a funny fish when you could be re-watching season one of *Homeland*. But what's even harder is a child that doesn't do well in his exams and ends up living with his parents all his life. Yikes. So, turn off the telly and give them all the help they need.

Discipline

I'm not saying you're a bad parent. After two months out of school, every other kid in the school is also addicted to whingeing and Haribo Jelly Babies. The problem is that they might find back to school a bit of an adjustment. That isn't your issue, until they go into Haribo Jelly Baby withdrawal in mid-September and get suspended for repeat whingeing. And now they're back in your house. So, wean them off the sugar and whingeing before things get out of hand.

4.9 I WANT TO CANCEL MOTHER'S DAY

Okay, we're close to the end of the book. I genuinely don't know how you found the time to read this far. Maybe you should write a book and tell us how you did it.

Before I sign off and go back to chasing around after my kids, I'd like to share a recent piece I wrote for the *Irish Examiner*. It's a bit of a rant about the way modern Dad doesn't get the credit that's due to him. And it all starts with Father's Day.

Here's the truth about Father's Day. It isn't just another Hallmark holiday, designed to sell cards and enrich people who make novelty socks. It's a special day, set aside in the calendar, where your family comes together to deliver the message that you aren't actually as important as Mom.

Put it this way – Mother's Day has a clear purpose. It's that one day of the year when we acknowledge Mom has done an incredible job under difficult circumstances. She usually gets the day off housework, some expensive chocolates and a bunch of flowers. There might be disappointment in some homes if she didn't also get a voucher for an expensive spa break. (That could be classed as 'taken for granted'. You don't want to go there.) You certainly wouldn't want to give her joke clothes or cheap jewellery. Mom wouldn't like that one bit.

And, yet, that's what Dad's going to get. Why? Because in the modern scheme of things, Dad is a complete eejit.

Now, I accept it's our own fault that we are viewed as eejits. Despite centuries of research, we still know only one thing for certain about women. The best way to attract one is to make her laugh. So, if you want to become a dad you will need to spend a lot of your adult life acting the eejit. But this notion of Mom raising the kids while Dad comes home from work and acts the clown is more out of date than sending someone a fax. It's a relic of a golden era for blokes, when our forefathers somehow persuaded our foremothers to stay at home with the kids while they were out at work, or maybe just listening to a match in the car. And what did the women get in return? Breakfast in bed once a year, served with a bunch of flowers from the petrol station. You have to say, it was a sweet deal for generations of men. And this current generation is the one left holding the bill.

Life has changed dramatically since I left home in 1989. Men aren't invisible on the home front any more. That's mainly because we stay living the single life well into our thirties. So, if we didn't know how to clean and cook for ourselves, we'd never get a partner, what with smelling like a farmyard and sporting man-boobs down to our knees. We are the most domesticated generation of men in history. There's even talk of a fella in Kildare who knows what should go into a wool wash.

With more men going the stay-at-home-dad route, it's time to recognise that Mom isn't the only parent in town. Some people have tried to address this by renaming Mother's Day as Mothering Sunday. Sorry, but Mothering Sunday sounds like a curse. ('Mothering Sunday!' says you, trying to avoid saying 'Shut the fuck up!' in front of the kids.)

There are two ways to handle this. One is to upgrade Father's Day and give us a decent present. Don't try that in your house, mainly because your kids haven't any money and you'll just end up footing the bill.

It would be far more sensible to downgrade Mother's Day, to show some parity of esteem. Better still, get rid of both of them altogether. I can't imagine any man crying into his pint over this. And I've never come across a woman who likes breakfast in bed. If any women out there yearn for something more imaginative, here's what I know about overly romantic men who make a lot of effort on the celebration front. They all have a mistress in Clonmel. (You won't see this in any official statistics.) So be careful what you wish for.

Anyway, rant over. Best of luck trying to abolish Mother and Father's Day in your house (seriously, everyone's a winner). If it doesn't pan out, then don't forget that you are in charge of organising Mother's Day for your partner. (Let's just say I'll never forget the year I forgot.)

Here are two options:

1. Get up without waking her and take the kids away for a week. Anything else will be a slight disappointment.

2. If that's not an option, you'll need a two-chocolate strategy. That's a box of something light to take her up to 3 p.m., and the full Milk Tray for when the kids are in bed. If either of these looks like the non-standard sizes you get in Dealz, you're toast. If they are clearly part of a multi-pack, you'll spend the whole day batting back questions you probably don't want to answer.

Finally, for any wives or partners reading this book, here is what we would like for Father's Day, in no particular order:

No socks or mugs.
A free pass to watch a match of our choice.
Sex.
Some more sex.

Look, we never said we were complicated.

THANKS FOR READING!

MERCIER PRESS

IRISH PUBLISHER - IRISH STORY

We hope you enjoyed this book.

Since 1944, Mercier Press has published books that have been critically important to Irish life and culture. Books that dealt with subjects that informed readers about Irish scholars, Irish writers, Irish history and Ireland's rich heritage.

We believe in the importance of providing accessible histories and cultural books for all readers and all who are interested in Irish cultural life.

Our website is the best place to find out more information about Mercier, our books, authors, news and the best deals on a wide variety of books. Mercier tracks the best prices for our books online and we seek to offer the best value to our customers.

Sign up on our website to receive updates and special offers.

www.mercierpress.ie
www.facebook.com/mercier.press
www.twitter.com/irishpublisher

Mercier Press, Unit 3b, Oak House, Bessboro Rd, Blackrock, Cork, Ireland